HOW TO BUILD STRONG BUSINESS CREDIT AND NEVER USE YOUR OWN MONEY AGAIN

DAVID WASHINGTON

Dedication

This book is dedicated to every entrepreneur who ever felt trapped by limited resources, overlooked by banks, or underestimated by the world.

To those who refuse to let their circumstances define their future, this is your blueprint.

May these pages give you the confidence, strategy, and courage to build something bigger than you ever imagined.

Contents

Introduction

The Key That Changes Everything

Let's get one thing straight before we go any further: This book is not about theory. It's about power. Real power that allows you to walk into a room and make moves because you've built something that can't be taken from you, financial leverage. Not the kind you get from cutting corners or maxing out personal credit cards to keep your business afloat, but the kind built through business credit, a hidden system most entrepreneurs never learn to use.

Imagine unlocking the secrets to true financial freedom, not the "get rich quick" stuff, but a legitimate path to growing your business without constantly draining your personal savings or begging banks to take a chance on you.

Imagine what it would feel like to finally have access to capital, opportunities, and partnerships, not because you came from money, but because you played the credit game like a pro.

That's exactly what this book is about.

This is your key.

Business credit is like a separation line, the thing that distinguishes entrepreneurs who constantly scrape by from those who scale effortlessly. It's what allows some people to take big swings, invest in their vision, and grow their empire, while others stay stuck, not because they aren't talented or driven, but because they never had access to the rules of the game.

I know this because I've lived it, and I'm writing this book for the hustlers and builders out there who are tired of being overlooked, underestimated, or just plain uninformed. The ones who want to break free from the paycheck-to-paycheck cycle or the small thinking that says, *"You can only grow if you already have money."* That's a lie.

The truth? You can grow when you understand credit and use it correctly.

Why Business Credit Matters More Than You Think

Business credit isn't just something nice to have; it's a game-changer. When you separate your personal credit from your business credit, you give your business room to breathe. Room to scale. Room to mess up, learn, and still recover, without wrecking your personal financial life in the process.

Think about it. Your personal credit was never designed to fund a business. It's based on how you handle car loans, credit cards, or personal debt, not how you manage inventory, payroll, or vendor accounts. Using personal credit for business expenses is like using a screwdriver to hammer nails; it might work for a while, but it's going to cause damage eventually.

Business credit is built differently on a separate system entirely. The best part? You don't need perfect personal credit to start.

Let me say that again: You do not need perfect personal credit to build business credit.

That's one of the biggest myths that holds people back, and it's one of the first we'll crush in this book.

Business credit levels the playing field. It gives you the ability to fund your dreams, not just survive. It opens doors to vendor relationships, credit cards with high limits, lines of credit, and loans that don't require a personal guarantee. It allows your business to stand on its own name, build its own reputation, and eventually attract investors, buyers, or partners who take you seriously, not because of your personal credit score, but because your business has its own track record.

This is how successful entrepreneurs scale without drowning in debt. This is how they protect their homes, families, and personal futures while still taking bold business risks. And this is what you're about to learn how to do.

Who This Book Is For

This book is for you... The ambitious professional who's ready to take control of their financial future and build something real.

Whether you're a startup founder with a dream, a side hustler looking to go full-time, a freelancer turning into a business owner, or a seasoned entrepreneur who never learned how credit works, this book will meet you exactly where you are.

Maybe you've never even heard of business credit before.

Maybe you've been denied funding too many times to count.

Maybe you’re tired of using your own money just to keep the lights on.

Maybe you're tired of being told "no."

Good. That means you're ready.

Once you understand how this system works and see the blueprint, you’ll realize it’s not about where you start. It’s about what you build. And I’m here to help you build something solid, scalable, and unstoppable.

A Roadmap You Can Actually Follow

If you’re like most people, the world of credit can feel overwhelming, like trying to navigate a foreign country without a map. You hear terms like *EIN, D-U-N-S Number, Net 30, trade references, Tier 1, Tier 3, secured lines, utilization ratios,* and your brain checks out before you even get started.

It’s not that you’re not smart enough. It’s that no one ever broke it down for you in plain English.

Well, that changes right here.

This book is designed to be the roadmap I wish someone had handed me when I was starting out. No fluff. No financial jargon. No high-level theory without real steps. Just honest, tested strategies written by someone who’s been in the trenches and built real credit from the ground up, without using personal money, without a trust fund, and without connections.

Every chapter in this book is like a rung on a ladder, lifting you from where you are now to where you want your business to be.

We start with the basics, how credit really works, and why business credit is a completely different game from personal credit. Then, step by step, I show you how to move from invisible to unstoppable.

Each piece connects to the next like clockwork. We'll build your foundation, establish your business identity, open credit files, utilize starter vendors to create a positive payment history, climb the credit tiers, and eventually unlock serious funding, all without impacting your personal credit profile.

You won't just learn *what* to do; you'll also learn why it works. You'll learn *how* it all connects. Most importantly, you'll know how to apply it to your unique situation, even if you're just getting started.

By the time you turn the last page, you'll know how to:

- Set up your business the right way from day one, so you're not backtracking or missing credibility points that lenders care about.

- Separate your personal and business finances to protect your personal assets and establish a distinct financial identity for your business.

- Register with credit bureaus and get your D-U-N-S Number, giving your business a seat at the credit table.

- Utilize Net 30 vendor accounts to establish a positive payment history, even if your business is new.

- Graduate to higher-tier store cards, fleet cards, and business credit cards that offer real spending power and flexibility.

- Avoid the hidden landmines that destroy your credit score before you even get a chance to build.
- Leverage your credit to grow your business, automate your systems, hire smarter, and scale with confidence.

This isn't abstract theory. This is a real, working system.

A system I've used myself.

A system that works for entrepreneurs, contractors, creators, freelancers, and small business owners across industries.

And most importantly, a system that doesn't require you to go into personal debt or beg a bank for a shot.

By the time you finish this book, you'll have a crystal-clear understanding of how to build business credit from zero, access funding without personal guarantees, and create a self-sustaining financial ecosystem for your business. A system that fuels your business while protecting your personal credit and peace of mind.

More Than Just Money

To be clear, this isn't just about money. This is about freedom.

It's about not being at the mercy of banks, investors, or people who don't see your vision.

It's about transitioning from survival mode to expansion mode.

It's about having the power to say yes when opportunity knocks, and not having to dip into your personal savings or max out your credit cards to make it happen.

This is a mindset shift.

Most of us were raised to think of credit as dangerous, something to avoid, something only "big businesses" use. However, the truth is that credit, when used strategically, isn't inherently dangerous. It's leverage. It's access. It's control.

This book is about flipping the script.

Because business credit isn't just a score, it's a signal.

It tells lenders whether or not you're trustworthy.

It tells suppliers whether or not to extend you better terms.

It tells investors whether or not your business is scalable.

And most importantly, it tells *you* whether or not you're building something sustainable or just winging it.

When you start building business credit the right way, you send a whole new signal:

That you're serious.

That you're organized.

That you're *here to win.*

And the doors that open because of that?

They're worth it.

Let's Get to Work

You won't find recycled Instagram quotes or generic finance tips dressed up to sound deep. On the other hand, this isn't a dense, overly technical manual written in corporate language either. I didn't write this to impress bankers. I wrote it to empower entrepreneurs like you, people who are driven, hungry, and ready to take control of their financial future.

What you're holding is a blueprint. If you follow it, one step at a time, it's going to transform the way you see and use credit in your business. You're not just going to learn how to build business credit. You'll understand how it works, how to manage it, and how to make it work for you.

By the time you finish, you'll have a working knowledge of how to establish, grow, and maintain strong business credit. You'll know exactly how to position your company to get approved for high-limit credit cards, vendor accounts, and even bank loans, all without touching your personal credit.

More importantly, you'll walk away with a real strategy, not just to access capital, but to build systems and structures that support long-term growth.

That's the big shift here. We're not just building credit. We're building leverage. We're moving you from hustling just to stay afloat to structuring your business like a real player, someone who's not just surviving, but scaling.

Once you understand how to use credit this way, you'll stop second-guessing every move. You won't hesitate to invest in growth, whether that means buying inventory, hiring help, upgrading equipment, or launching a new product.

You'll stop pulling money out of your own pocket, maxing out personal cards, or worrying about how you'll fund the next step.

Instead, you'll know how to tap into resources designed specifically for your business. You'll make confident decisions because they're backed by a foundation you built with intention. You'll stop playing small, because you'll no longer be waiting for permission to grow.

And maybe most important of all, you'll stop asking yourself whether or not you're ready.

Because here's the truth, you are ready. If you've made it this far, if you're reading this with even a flicker of belief that your business can be something more, then the next step is already calling your name.

You don't need perfect credit, a finance degree, or a massive team. You just need the right information, the willingness to apply it, and the courage to act.

This book gives you the information. The rest? That's on you.

It's time to take the mystery out of business credit and replace it with clarity and control.

Build a system that works for you, not just today, but for the long haul.

Create something that lasts, something that grows with you and opens doors instead of closing them.

By the end of this journey, you won't just understand business credit but also own it. You'll control it. You'll be able to use it as a tool to build the kind of business and the kind of life you've been working toward all along.

This is where it begins.

Time to build.

Chapter 01: The Language Of Credit

The Hidden Risk of Using Personal Credit for Business

Your personal credit tells a story, your story. It tracks how you manage money in your day-to-day life. Credit cards, car payments, student loans, your mortgage, it's all there. Every time you swipe a card, apply for financing, or miss a due date, that activity becomes part of your personal credit report. It's linked to your Social Security number and sticks with you for years. It's how banks decide whether to lend you money for a new car, a house, or even approve a basic credit card.

And when you're not running a business, that's fine. That system works. But the second you start putting business expenses on your personal cards, or using your own credit to fund your company's growth, that's where things can get messy fast.

Now imagine using that same personal reputation to run a business. Let's say your business needs a new laptop, a $10,000 inventory order, or even a delivery van. If you're putting that on a personal credit card or co-signing a lease with your Social Security number, then your private financial identity is now exposed to business risks. If anything goes wrong, a slow season, a supply chain delay, a client who never pays, you're on the hook personally. That can mean wrecked credit, drained savings, and an uphill battle just to get back to where you started.

Business credit, on the other hand, exists to prevent exactly that. It's not tied to your personal credit score or Social Security number, but instead to your business's EIN (Employer Identification Number) and DUNS number. When properly set up, your company becomes a separate financial entity, capable of building its own credit profile, qualifying for loans, applying for trade lines, and securing leases or vendor relationships without ever touching your personal credit. This separation isn't just clean bookkeeping; it's a shield. A line of protection between your business risks and your personal life.

Once that structure is in place, your business can begin to grow in ways that your personal credit never could support.

Why Personal Credit Can't Power Business Growth

Most people don't realize how limited personal credit actually is when it comes to funding a business. It's not just about the smaller limits or higher interest rates, although those are very real. The issue runs deeper.

The personal credit system was never designed for business use. It's meant to track the financial habits of individuals, not companies. So when you use your personal credit to float your business, even for something as small as a few startup purchases, you're stretching a tool beyond what it was built for. The result? You hit walls faster. Credit utilization spikes and your score drops. Your ability to qualify for a home mortgage, refinance debt, or even get a car loan can be negatively affected just because you were trying to grow a business.

It's a lose-lose situation: your personal credit gets strained, and your business remains stuck under its shadow.

Business credit, however, is built for scale. Vendor accounts, net-30 terms, fleet financing, high-limit business credit cards, these are tools that businesses can use without overleveraging personal assets. And as your business proves it can handle its obligations by paying on time, managing credit responsibly, and staying in good standing, its credit profile strengthens. That growing profile unlocks more opportunities: better terms, larger loans, more favorable contracts, and even credibility with partners or investors. In many ways, business credit becomes a growth engine, quietly compounding your ability to expand without relying on your personal resources.

Why Most Entrepreneurs Miss This Step

Of course, the biggest hurdle for most people isn't structure; it's mindset. A lot of aspiring entrepreneurs never even consider business credit because they're trapped by outdated information, or worse, misinformation.

There's a whole world of myths that circulate, especially online. Maybe you've heard a few of them.

"You need excellent personal credit to get started."

"You can't build business credit unless you've been in business for years."

"Business credit isn't real unless you have a massive company."

"If you're a sole proprietor or an LLC with one member, none of this applies to you."

All false.

The truth is, you can begin building business credit without perfect personal credit, and in fact, many people do. Lenders and vendors often base their decisions on your business's credit profile, not yours, especially when your business is structured properly, and you've started establishing trade lines or vendor accounts. There are entire systems built around this, designed to help even small startups or single-member LLCs create a strong business credit history.

Another myth is that you have to wait until you're making money to start building credit. But just like with personal credit, the key is starting early. You don't build a solid score by waiting; you build it by engaging with the system in smart, low-risk ways. Paying on time, using vendor credit responsibly, applying for low-limit business cards and proving your reliability. These small steps add up, and the sooner you begin, the more leverage you'll have when you truly need it.

Ultimately, the truth is simple: you don't need to be perfect, you just need to be intentional. Business credit is real, it's powerful, and it's available. Once you understand how it works, you'll never go back to running everything through your personal credit again.

Let's start with the one belief that quietly keeps so many business owners frozen in place, the myth that you must have excellent personal credit before you can even begin thinking about building business credit.

It sounds logical, especially if you've spent years being told your credit score is the only thing lenders care about. And for personal loans, mortgages, and individual credit cards, that might be true. But when it comes to business credit? It's a different ballgame. Your personal credit and your business credit are not permanently tied together. In fact, one of the core reasons business credit even exists is to separate your company's financial life from your own.

This myth, that personal perfection is a prerequisite, creates paralysis. People hold off on registering an LLC, opening vendor accounts, or applying for a business credit card because they think, *"Why bother? My score is too low; no one will approve me."* What they don't realize is that there are systems already in place to help new businesses build credit from the ground up, no matter what your personal credit looks like.

And here's the twist: some business lenders and vendors never even check your personal score. What they care about is how your business handles its obligations, whether invoices are paid on time, whether you've established trade lines, and whether your business is in good standing with relevant reporting agencies. That's it. It's less about who you are as a borrower and more about whether your business can be trusted.

The people who break through this myth and take action early, even while their personal credit is still in recovery, often gain access to opportunities others don't. They build vendor relationships faster. They get net-30 terms without a personal guarantee. They stop putting expenses on personal cards. And over time, their business becomes its own financial force, untethered from past personal mistakes.

Your Credit Behavior Is Your Business Reputation

It's easy to think of credit as something reactive. You apply when you need money, and that's when it matters, right? Not exactly. What's more true is that your business's credit behavior is like a living track record, a history that tells potential lenders, vendors, and partners what kind of operation you're running, long before you ask them for anything.

For example, say you've got a few vendor accounts open. You're buying supplies on net-30 terms and consistently paying early. That behavior gets recorded. Not just internally, it gets reported to credit agencies like Experian Business, Equifax Business, and Dun & Bradstreet. Over time, that history becomes the foundation of your business credit profile. And once you've got a strong profile, doors start opening, not because you're asking, but because you've proven yourself to be low-risk.

Suddenly, suppliers start offering you better terms. You may get invited into partner programs. A credit card issuer might pre-approve your business for a higher limit. You go from pitching yourself to being approached, because your history speaks louder than your application ever could.

Credit behavior is influenced. It's not just about what you *need* today. It's about what you *unlock* tomorrow, simply by being responsible and consistent. Even small habits, such as paying on time, keeping balances low, and not overextending, add up in powerful ways. And in business, where trust and reliability are everything, those patterns can elevate you from just another company to a business worth betting on.

This brings us to one of the most underrated effects of strong business credit: the ripple effect.

People often focus on the immediate benefits, getting a loan, qualifying for a card, and opening a vendor account, but they miss the longer-term compounding results. When your business credit is in good shape, it doesn't just help you borrow money. It improves the overall reputation of your business.

Take vendor relationships, for example. When a supplier sees that you pay early or on time every month, they're more likely to extend better terms. Maybe they offer net-60 instead of net-30. Maybe they will increase your limit. Maybe they flag you as a preferred customer. And because vendors talk, and many of them report to credit agencies, strong behavior starts showing up across the board.

Next thing you know, you've got better terms from shipping partners, software providers, and material suppliers, all because your reputation precedes you. And it's not just the vendors who notice.

Investors and lenders look at business credit when assessing whether your company is financially stable. If your credit profile is strong, it signals that your business can manage its money, honor its commitments, and plan ahead, all key ingredients for scaling. That trust translates to higher business valuation. Your company becomes more attractive not just as a borrower, but as a potential partner, acquisition, or investment.

Even when it comes time to exit or sell the business, a strong credit history becomes a valuable asset. Buyers see it as a sign that they're walking into a well-run, low-risk operation. And that alone can elevate the terms of a deal.

So no, credit isn't just about money. It's about motion. Momentum. It's the reputation your business builds in the background that ultimately shapes the trajectory of everything else.

When you treat credit as a strategic tool, not a reactive one, the ripple effects start to show up everywhere. From the vendors you work with, to the capital you qualify for, to the long-term stability of your business itself.

It's one thing to talk about credit in theory, to discuss scores, limits, and vendor terms like abstract tools in a toolkit. But the impact of business credit becomes much more real when you see how others have used it, sometimes in moments of survival, other times to scale faster than they thought possible.

There's the story of Maya, a small catering business owner in Atlanta, who started with a folding table, three recipes, and a fire in her belly. She had no savings, and her personal credit was shot from a divorce that left her picking up the financial pieces. But she registered an LLC, got a free DUNS number, opened a couple of net-30 vendor accounts for food packaging and cleaning supplies, and paid them like clockwork. Six months later, she had a business credit score. Within a year, she secured a small equipment lease and a business credit card, both in the company's name, without anyone asking for her Social Security number.

Those early trade lines may not have seemed glamorous, but they built a foundation that allowed her to lease a small commercial kitchen space. From there, she got into local markets, then small corporate gigs. By year three, she had contracts with two hospitals, a staff of eight, and her own delivery van, financed entirely through her business.

What changed? Not luck. Not a windfall. Just credit, used strategically.

Then there's Jay, a graphic designer who freelanced for years and always felt stuck. His clients paid late. His invoices floated unpaid for weeks. He wanted to grow, maybe bring on a part-time assistant or invest in better equipment, but every time he looked at his personal finances, the numbers said "not yet."

He never thought to build business credit. Honestly, he didn't know it was even a thing. But once he got structured, switched to an S-Corp, opened a business checking account, and applied for a few vendor lines with online design tools and office suppliers, things began to change. His business credit profile grew, and that opened up access to funding that didn't come with 24% personal card interest. Within eighteen months, Jay was able to finance a studio space and hire his first contractor.

Credit didn't change who Jay was as a creative. It just gave him room to move, to stop surviving invoice to invoice and start planning six months ahead. That space made all the difference.

Business Credit: Your Silent Growth Engine

Stories like these aren't rare. They just aren't often told. Business credit isn't loud or flashy, but it's powerful. And one of its most underrated features is the business credit score itself.

Most entrepreneurs have never even seen their business credit score. Fewer still know what goes into it. But banks, suppliers, commercial landlords, leasing companies, and even potential partners are often looking at it in the background. It's your company's resume. And just like a resume, it tells a story, not just about what you've done, but how reliable you've been while doing it.

A strong score signals more than repayment. It shows consistency. It shows accountability. And it shows that your business has learned how to operate within financial agreements, which, in today's economy, is a rare and valuable trait.

With a healthy business credit profile, you're not just applying for funding anymore; you're often being pre-qualified or even courted. Vendors offer better terms without you asking. Leasing agents call back faster. Lenders propose higher limits with better interest rates. That one number quietly works for you behind the scenes, day after day, softening friction where it would otherwise slow you down.

And here's something not enough people say: business credit can also improve how *you* feel about running your company. When you're constantly using personal funds, everything feels fragile. You're one bad month away from crisis. But once your business has its own weight, its own profile, its own credit identity, it feels more real. More stable. More professional. And that shift in mindset? That's when momentum begins.

The truth is, many people view credit as a last resort. A burden. Something you turn to only when you've run out of options or need to fix a cash problem. But the smartest business owners use it very differently.

They see it as a strategic asset, not something to avoid, but something to understand and wield. They use credit to buy time, to expand capacity, to negotiate better deals. They use it to build trust in the marketplace. And they use it to protect their personal stability while allowing the business to grow on its own two feet.

If you're still seeing credit as something to fear or fight with, you're likely carrying the old model, the reactive one, where debt equals danger. But in today's business world, access is everything. Liquidity creates leverage. And leverage, used wisely, is how you scale, how you protect, and how you stay in control.

By the end of this chapter, your mindset should begin to shift. You don't need to chase perfection or wait for someone else to give you permission. You just need to start seeing credit not as a weight, but as a lever, something you can move, use, and build with. Once you do that, a whole new set of doors starts to appear.

And when they open, you'll be ready.

Chapter 02: Forming A Legitimate Business

Choosing Your Business Structure Wisely

Before building credit, before applying for a single loan or vendor account, you must start where the system begins, with a legal business entity. The structure you choose becomes the framework that defines how the government, banks, and credit bureaus will perceive your company.

This is about how much personal risk you're taking on, how seriously lenders view your business, and what kind of funding options you'll be eligible for down the line. A sole proprietorship might be the easiest to start, but it doesn't offer any legal separation between you and your business. That matters more than you think. If the business gets sued or falls into debt, you will be personally liable.

In contrast, a corporation offers more protection but adds complexity, including more rules, increased oversight, and reduced agility. That's the tradeoff. And whichever path you choose, know this: your legal setup quietly sets the terms for every future conversation with lenders, suppliers, and agencies. It's the invisible script they'll use to decide how far they'll trust you, and how much they'll invest.

Why (Limited Liability Company) LLCs Hit the Balance

For most entrepreneurs, especially solo founders or small teams, LLCs offer a practical middle ground. They're widely recognized as separate legal entities, which means you get personal liability protection, just like a corporation. But unlike a corporation, you aren't buried under layers of formal meetings, officer roles, or corporate resolutions.

Credit bureaus and lenders see LLCs as legitimate, established entities. They show up in state records, have formal operating agreements, and make your business look "real" in ways that matter on paper. That perception can open doors. Many vendors, lenders, and partners hesitate when a business is structured as a sole proprietorship because there's no clear separation between the owner and the entity. An LLC helps you clear that hurdle from the beginning.

Plus, there's flexibility in how you're taxed. LLCs can be treated as sole proprietorships, partnerships, or even S corporations, depending on your situation and growth stage. That optionality makes it easier to adapt over time without overhauling your business setup every time your income changes.

The Registration Walkthrough

Turning a concept into a legally recognized business involves a few specific steps. And while it may sound bureaucratic, each one serves a purpose in establishing your business for future credibility.

It begins with selecting a name that fits your brand, is legally available in your state, and meets official naming requirements. That name becomes your business's legal identity, the one that appears on your state filings, tax records, vendor accounts, and credit profiles.

Next, you'll file what's called the *Articles of Organization* with your state's business division (usually the Secretary of State). This document formally creates your LLC. During that filing, you'll also need to name a registered agent, a person or service that can legally accept documents on your behalf.

A small filing fee is usually required, and once approved, you'll receive confirmation that your LLC is active. At this point, your business becomes a separate legal entity, distinct from you as an individual.

While these steps might seem technical, they carry weight. Lenders and credit agencies reference these records when verifying your legitimacy. Done right, this process creates a solid first impression and ensures you're not doubling back later to fix credibility issues that could have been avoided from the start.

The Standards Lenders Actually Look For

When credit agencies examine a business, they don't care about your hustle or intentions. They look for structure, consistency, and signs of credibility that match their internal checklists. These aren't suggestions, they're pass/fail requirements.

Is the business officially filed? That's just the beginning. What's the listed phone number, and is it registered under the business name? Does your email end in a branded domain, or are you still using a personal Gmail account? What's the business address, and is it commercial, virtual, or residential? These are the kinds of things that separate a verified operation from something that feels like it's still being run out of a garage.

Meeting these standards early creates less friction later. When lenders review your file, and all the details align, including business name, EIN, address, phone, and domain, they're more likely to approve. Discrepancies, on the other hand, slow everything down or shut it off entirely.

Getting Your EIN, And Getting It Right

Your EIN is the key that unlocks the financial side of your business. No EIN, no bank account. No lending. No credit file. That number becomes the thread tying together every major step: registration, taxes, credit, and funding.

And yet, it's common for businesses to mess this up. Applying under the wrong name, listing a mismatched address, skipping steps to save time, those shortcuts end up causing delays, denials, and data mismatches across systems. Fixing it later is harder than doing it right the first time.

The EIN application is free. The cost of getting it wrong is not.

Your Financial Fingerprint

Once assigned, your EIN becomes more than just a number; it becomes the fingerprint lenders use to track your entire business history. Every application, every payment history, every trade account opened in your company's name ties back to that ID.

Think of it this way: your EIN is the key that unlocks access to the financial building where your business will grow. But if the information tied to it is inconsistent, wrong name, outdated address, or mismatched phone, it triggers flags at every checkpoint. A single digit or detail out of place can block approvals you were otherwise eligible for.

The way you set up your business tells a story, one that lenders and credit bureaus will keep reading. Clean, consistent documentation is what positions your business for funding, credibility, and long-term growth.

Virtual Address, Real Impact

There's something subtle, but powerful, about the image your business presents on paper. One of the fastest ways to influence how banks, lenders, and credit agencies perceive your operation is through the address you choose to associate with it. And while it might seem like a small detail, using the wrong type of address can quietly sabotage your credibility before you ever make it to the application stage.

That's where virtual addresses come in, not as a convenience, but as a strategic asset.

When starting, most entrepreneurs naturally default to using a home address. After all, the business is being run from there. But that choice, practical as it may be, sends signals that credit bureaus and underwriters don't like. It suggests a side hustle, not a scalable entity. It implies informality. And unfortunately, it can become a red flag.

On the other hand, virtual addresses allow you to present your business with the professionalism of a downtown office suite, even if you're building from your kitchen table. We're not talking about fake shell locations or mailbox drops. The best virtual address services provide access to real, commercial spaces, complete with offices, staff, signage, and mail-handling services. More importantly, these addresses are recognized and accepted by institutions that issue credit and review business legitimacy.

The perception shift matters. A business listing tied to a commercial address indicates to lenders that you're serious. It suggests planning, structure, and presence. And when that address is matched across your business registration, EIN, bank account, credit applications, and online listings, it builds a consistency that underwriters and data systems look for.

Aligning your business with professional standards from the beginning saves you from costly corrections down the road. It's easier to build right the first time than to rebuild later.

The Wrong Address Can Cost You

Let's be clear: some addresses can block your progress before you even know there's an issue.

Many lenders, especially those using automated approval systems, are programmed to flag or deny applications associated with P.O. boxes or residential addresses. And it's not just banks. Vendor accounts, business credit cards, and even government registrations can trigger friction if the business address doesn't appear valid or professional in the backend systems they check against.

Here's why: When an address is tied to a personal residence, the business is seen as unstable or unserious. The thinking is simple: if it's easy to shut down, hard to find, or likely part-time, it's riskier to lend to. The same goes for mailbox stores like UPS or USPS drop locations. Although these provide street addresses, their metadata is often flagged in credit review systems, marking them as non-commercial.

And once that flag is in your profile, removing it isn't simple.

Switching your address later doesn't always fix your file. Historical records and automated scraping tools can continue to associate your business with its original registration location, meaning your credibility is compromised even after you've upgraded.

That's why starting strong matters. Choose a virtual address from a reputable provider, one with real offices, consistent listings, and no history of being blacklisted by banks. Ensure the address is displayed on your website, registration documents, and all online and offline platforms where your business operates. That level of alignment helps create a smooth credit-building experience. It reduces denials. It creates trust. And trust is currency.

Building the Right Way, Not Just the Easy Way

When you're laying the foundation of your business, there are two paths you can take: fast or right.

Doing it fast means filling out forms, skipping details, and figuring things out as you go. Doing it right means starting with intention, choosing the correct structure, registering with care, establishing a professional presence, and setting up your credit infrastructure from the outset.

This chapter is your shortcut to doing it right.

You'll understand how each piece of your setup connects to the next. You'll see why obtaining your EIN matters beyond just tax purposes. You'll learn how your address, phone number, and email work together to either strengthen or weaken your business credibility. You'll be able to avoid the quiet mistakes most entrepreneurs don't discover until a lender explains why their application was denied.

More importantly, you'll stop seeing registration as mere paperwork and start recognizing it as a positioning tool.

Positioning for partnerships. Positioning for approvals. Positioning for growth.

Scores matter, but recognition matters more. Your business is recognized as legitimate by systems that don't know you personally. They're not looking at your hustle, your dreams, or your story. They're looking at your setup, and that's what this chapter equips you to master.

Confidence Starts With Foundation

The difference between a business that struggles and one that grows often comes down to the foundation it was built on. When you know your business is properly structured, with every detail aligned and every document consistent, you enter funding conversations with clarity. You apply for accounts knowing you're qualified, not guessing.

There's a kind of peace in that.

You won't have to worry about your application being denied due to a technicality. You won't find yourself redoing forms because your address doesn't match the one on your registration. You won't need to explain to a lender why your business doesn't have a bank account or why your EIN has the wrong contact info.

Instead, you'll focus on what matters: building.

That's the goal of this chapter. Not to impress you with terminology or overwhelm you with tasks, but to give you structure. Clarity. A checklist you can actually use.

When you take the time to build your business properly at the foundation level, everything that comes after, vendor accounts, credit tiers, high-limit cards, and lines of credit, unfolds more naturally. And when setbacks come (because they always do), you'll be standing on something solid.

You're not just setting up a company.

You're building something lenders trust, clients respect, and you can stand behind with confidence.

That's how you build for the long run. That's how you grow, right?

Chapter 03: Setting The Foundation

Opening a Business Bank Account

When it comes to starting a business, our mind often conjures images of fun activities such as drafting a logo, drawing customers, or making the first sale. Little do most new entrepreneurs realise that one of the most significant, albeit often missed, steps in building a real, fundable company doesn't involve any of the aforementioned activities at all. It is something that sounds as simple as opening a bank account for the company.

At first, it may not sound like a big deal. After all, couldn't you just run everything through your personal checking account, especially if you're just testing the waters? On the surface, that feels easier and maybe even more efficient. But here's the hard truth: if you're serious about creating a business that banks, lenders, and investors will take

seriously, you need to separate your finances from day one. And the way you do that is by establishing a dedicated business bank account.

Why a Business Bank Account Matters

Think of your business like a house. You can decorate it however you like, but without a strong foundation, everything built on top of it is unstable. A business bank account is part of that foundation. It's more than a convenient place to deposit checks and pay bills. It's the line in the sand that says, "This is not just me hustling on the side. This is a legitimate company."

Lenders and credit bureaus recognize that distinction immediately. When they look at a business, one of the first things they check is whether there's a separate bank account tied to the company. If they don't see one, your business risks looking like a hobby instead of a serious operation. And in their eyes, hobbies don't get funding.

But the benefits don't stop with appearances. A business bank account is also critical for legal and tax purposes. By separating your money, you protect your personal assets in case your business ever faces legal issues. Without that separation, there's a chance a court could decide that your business is just an extension of you personally, putting everything you own, your car, your savings, even your home, at risk.

From a tax perspective, having all your income and expenses flowing through a single business account saves you countless headaches when it's time to file. Instead of digging through personal transactions and trying to remember which dinner was a client meeting and which was just pizza night with friends, everything is cleanly recorded.

What You'll Need to Open One

Opening a business bank account isn't complicated, but you do need to come prepared.

Most banks will require three basic things:

1. **Your business formation documents** – These prove that your company actually exists. If you've formed an LLC, for example, you'll need your Articles of Organization. If you're running a corporation, you'll need your Articles of Incorporation.
2. **Your EIN (Employer Identification Number)** – Think of this as a Social Security number for your business. You can get one directly from the IRS, and it's completely free. Even if you don't plan to hire employees right away, an EIN signals that your business is a separate entity.
3. **Your business address** – Banks want to know that your business has a physical or at least official presence. This doesn't always mean you need a fancy office; a virtual business address or even a coworking space address can often work.

Once you've gathered these, the process itself is fairly straightforward. You walk into a bank (or apply online), submit the paperwork, and your account is opened. But while the process may be simple, choosing the right bank is worth a little thought.

Choosing the Right Bank

Not all banks are created equal, especially when it comes to small businesses.

You want to pick a bank that does two things:

1. **Reports to business credit bureaus.** Not every bank does this, and if they don't, you miss out on one of the biggest benefits of having a business account in the first place: building your credit profile. Make sure the bank you choose reports to agencies like Dun & Bradstreet, Equifax Business, or Experian Business.

2. **Offers tools for growth.** Some banks provide additional services like merchant accounts, business credit cards, or integration with accounting software. These tools make running your business smoother and prepare you for the next stages of growth.

While it may be tempting to stick with the same bank you use personally, don't choose convenience over strategy. Shop around, compare fees, and pay attention to the long-term benefits of each option.

Avoid the Common Mistake

Many new entrepreneurs decide to skip this step and use their personal accounts instead. Maybe they're trying to save on fees, or maybe they think they're too small for it to matter. But here's the problem: when you mix personal and business finances, you send the wrong signal to the people who could help you grow. To a bank officer reviewing a loan application, it looks messy and unprofessional. To an investor, it raises doubts about your financial management.

Even worse, running your business through personal accounts can disqualify you from funding altogether. Some lenders won't even consider your application if they don't see a dedicated business bank account.

Building Legitimacy and Access to Credit

When you do open your account, you're not just solving a bookkeeping issue; you're laying the groundwork for future opportunities. That account becomes the channel through which you can apply for business credit cards, lines of credit, and eventually, loans. It shows financial institutions that your company is operating as a true business entity, and that makes them more willing to extend resources to you.

Think of it as opening a door. Without it, you're locked out of most forms of business financing. With it, you gain access to essential financial products that can help your company scale.

The First Step Toward Growth

It's easy to underestimate how big a difference this one step makes. But separating your personal and business money changes the way you see your company. When you have a business bank account, you start treating your business with more seriousness, and so does everyone else.

In many ways, this single decision shapes the trajectory of your business. It's not glamorous. You won't post about it on social media. But behind the scenes, it's the move that transforms your side project into something real, fundable, and scalable.

So before you spend another dollar from your personal debit card, stop and ask yourself: Is this how a legitimate business would operate? If the answer is no, it's time to head to the bank and open that account. Because until you do, you haven't truly built the foundation your business deserves.

Separating Personal and Business Finances

One of the most common mistakes entrepreneurs make in their early days is mixing personal and business money. At first, it may not feel like a big deal. You're just starting out, so swiping your personal card for supplies or depositing customer payments into your personal account feels harmless. In fact, it might even feel easier, one account, one card, less hassle.

But here's the truth: that shortcut is one of the fastest ways to sabotage your business before it has a chance to grow. Mixing your finances creates confusion, damages your credibility, and in some cases, puts everything you own personally at risk. If you want your company to be taken seriously by lenders, credit bureaus, and even future investors, you must draw a bold line between your money and your business's money.

The Hidden Cost of Mixing Money

On the surface, combining accounts seems simple. But the problems start showing up when you need to make sense of your numbers. Suddenly, bookkeeping becomes a nightmare. You find yourself scrolling through bank statements, trying to figure out if that $85 charge was a business lunch with a client or just a family dinner. That one gray area multiplies into dozens of transactions, and by the time tax season rolls around, you're buried in receipts and guesswork.

But bookkeeping headaches are only the beginning. The much bigger issue is liability. Imagine your business faces a lawsuit or a major debt. If your personal and business finances are tangled together, courts can rule that your business is not a truly separate entity. That means your personal savings, your home, and even your car could be on the line. This is called "piercing the corporate veil," and once it happens, the whole reason you created a legal business structure (like an LLC or corporation) can be undermined.

Mixing money also hurts your credibility in the eyes of banks. When a lender sees that you're paying business bills from your personal checking account or that client payments are landing in the same account you use to pay your rent, it sends a clear message: this person isn't operating as a professional business owner. And when they doubt your professionalism, they also doubt your fundability.

The Mindset Shift

Separating finances is not just about paperwork; it's a mindset. It's the act of telling yourself and the world: *This is not just me. This is my business, and it stands on its own.*

The moment you commit to treating your business like an independent entity, your decision-making shifts. You begin to see expenses differently, track revenue with more intention, and build habits that mirror those of established companies. This separation isn't just financial, it's psychological. And that shift is what prepares you for growth.

Best Practices for Separation

So how do you actually keep things separate in a way that protects your business and builds credibility?

Here are a few practical steps every entrepreneur should take:

1. **Use your business bank account for everything.** Once your account is open, make it the hub for all business

transactions. Client payments, supplier invoices, subscriptions, everything flows in and out of that account.

2. **Get a business debit or credit card.** This card is for business purchases only. No groceries, no family dinners, no personal shopping. The card becomes a tool for tracking expenses and building your business credit profile.

3. **Pay yourself a salary or draw.** Instead of dipping into business funds whenever you need cash, establish a system where you pay yourself regularly, just like you'd pay an employee. This keeps the lines clean and prevents personal expenses from sneaking into business accounts.

4. **Never pay business expenses with personal funds.** If your business doesn't have enough cash at the moment, transfer money into the business account first, then use that account to make the payment. This maintains a clear paper trail that shows separation.

By following these practices, you not only protect yourself legally but also demonstrate professionalism to banks, partners, and potential investors.

Why Separation Matters for Taxes

Taxes are often where the benefits of clean separation really shine. When your business finances are isolated, tax preparation becomes significantly easier. You can pull reports directly from your business account and know with certainty that every line item is business-related. There's no second-guessing, no messy overlap.

This clarity also helps if you're ever audited. Instead of scrambling to prove which purchases were business expenses, you can simply point to your business account and show that it was used exclusively for company activity. This kind of clean recordkeeping not only reduces stress but also builds trust with tax authorities and financial institutions alike.

Building Fundability

Perhaps the most important reason to separate personal and business finances is fundability, the ability for your business to qualify for credit and loans. Banks and credit bureaus want to see that your company operates as an independent entity. They want to see dedicated accounts, clean records, and proof of income that isn't tied to your personal life.

When your finances are separate, you can produce financial statements that actually reflect your business performance. This makes it far easier to prove revenue, apply for credit, and gain access to the capital you'll eventually need to grow. Without separation, your applications may stall out, no matter how profitable your business actually is.

Confidence in Growth

An emotional benefit that gets very little talk is confidence. Knowing that your finances are clean, organized, and clearly separated gives you a certain sense of control in the day-to-day dealings of running your business. This gives you confidence to sit across from a banker, partner, or investor, knowing your business has been managed competently.

That very sense of legitimacy translates into how people see you. Once others see that you have taken the steps of running yourself like a true business, they will treat you as one. And that change in perception places obstacles in your way that would have never existed before.

The Bottom Line

Separating personal and business finances is not glamorous, and definitely does not feel fun at this point. However, it is one of those very unsexy behind-the-scenes maneuverings that serve to set up the conditioning for your company to either transition to sustainability or wrestle with utter confusion and risk.

By keeping everything clean and separate, you're doing more than following good financial practice. You're protecting yourself legally, making tax time easier, building fundability, and giving your business the credibility it needs to thrive.

So, if you're tempted to swipe your personal card for "just one" business purchase, stop and think: is that $50 charge worth risking the legitimacy of your business? If the answer is no, and it should be, then draw the line today. Separate your finances, and in doing so, give your business the foundation it needs to grow with confidence.

Building a Professional Business Identity

If you've ever looked at a business and thought, *"That feels official,"* chances are it wasn't just the product or service that gave you that impression. It was the details, the email address, the website, even the phone number, that told you this company was real. Those details may seem small, but they add up to credibility. And credibility is what separates a side project from a business that others want to partner with, invest in, or lend money to.

First Impressions Matter

Banks, suppliers, and credit bureaus don't know you personally. They don't get to see how hard you work, how committed you are, or what vision you carry for the future. All they can judge is what's in front of them. If the email on your application says "johnnybiz123@gmail.com," it instantly raises a flag. It suggests the business isn't fully established yet.

Now, that doesn't mean Gmail or Yahoo addresses are "bad." Millions of people use them. But in business credit and funding, perception matters. A professional email linked to your own domain, like **info@yourbusiness.com**, signals that you're serious. It says you've invested in the basics, and you're not just running things from your living room on a whim.

The Phone Number Factor

The same is true with phone numbers. If your company's contact number is the same line your family uses, it can feel unpolished to outsiders. Imagine a lender calling, and a child picks up. It's not a dealbreaker, but it chips away at the image you're trying to build. Setting up a dedicated business phone line solves this instantly.

Thankfully, it doesn't have to be expensive. Services like RingCentral, Grasshopper, or even simple VoIP apps give you a professional number that routes calls to your phone without exposing your personal line. Some even let you choose a toll-free number or a local area code, depending on how you want your business to appear.

That one small change, having a separate phone number, tells anyone dealing with you that this is a real operation, not just a personal project.

Owning Your Online Presence

Then there's your website and domain. In today's world, a business without a website raises eyebrows. People expect to type your name into a search bar and find something. If they don't, they start to wonder: Is this business legitimate?

Buying a domain is one of the cheapest, fastest steps you can take to solidify your identity. For the cost of a couple of coffees each month, you can own yourbusiness.com and use it not only for a website but also for branded email addresses. That domain becomes your digital storefront, even if you're not running an online business.

A simple, professional website doesn't need to be complicated. A homepage, a contact page, and maybe a short description of your services are enough to start. The goal isn't to impress people with design; it's to prove you exist and that you've put thought into presenting yourself.

Why Lenders Care

You might wonder why banks and credit bureaus even care about phone numbers or email addresses. After all, shouldn't they be more focused on revenue and cash flow? The truth is, they look at everything. Professional identity is one of the signals they use to measure risk.

If your contact information looks like something a hobbyist would set up in a few minutes, it makes them question how long the business will last. But if they see a dedicated number, a branded email, and a professional website, it creates confidence. They assume you're building something meant to endure. And when they feel confident, they're more likely to extend credit.

More Than Just Appearances

This isn't only about lenders. A polished identity affects how clients, suppliers, and even potential partners view you. A supplier is more likely to grant you favorable terms if they see you as a stable, established business. A partner feels more comfortable collaborating when your communication looks professional.

And perhaps most importantly, *you* feel the difference. When you sign into an email with your own domain or answer calls on your business line, it shifts your mindset. It reinforces the idea that you're running a company, not just doing a side hustle.

Small Investment, Big Impact

The good news is, these upgrades don't cost much. A domain might be $10–$15 a year. Business email hosting can be as low as a few dollars a month. Virtual phone numbers often start around the same price. For less than the cost of a night out, you can set up the infrastructure that positions your business as legitimate in the eyes of the people who matter most.

It's not about making your company look bigger than it is. It's about making it look *real*. A lender or supplier isn't expecting a startup to look like a Fortune 500 firm. They just want to see that you've taken the steps to separate your personal life from your professional identity.

Setting Yourself Up for Growth

Think of these elements, phone, email, and domain, as the finishing touches on the foundation you've been laying. Your business bank account and clean financial separation created the structure. These professional details decorate it with the signals of credibility. Together, they create a picture of a business that's prepared for growth.

And once those pieces are in place, opportunities start to open. You're in a stronger position to apply for business credit cards, request loans, and negotiate with suppliers. You're more likely to be taken seriously by clients who might otherwise hesitate to trust a new business.

Final Thoughts

The steps we've covered in this section don't require advanced skills or huge investments. They're simple, practical moves that any entrepreneur can take. But don't let their simplicity fool you. The impact they have on your credibility, fundability, and confidence is massive.

When you build a professional identity, a separate phone number, a branded email, and a clean website, you give your business a voice. You give it a presence. You give it a chance to stand on its own, not just as a reflection of you, but as an entity that can grow, attract funding, and earn respect.

In the end, it's about trust. Trust from lenders. Trust from partners. Trust yourself. And trust, once earned, is what allows a business to move forward and expand with confidence.

Chapter 04: The Credit Profile That Matters

Understanding Your Business Credit and the D-U-N-S Number

Okay, before we dive into the boring-looking numbers and scores, let's get one thing straight: your business credit is your business's reputation on paper. It's how banks, lenders, and even vendors decide whether they can trust you with money, credit, or opportunities. Think of it like this: if your business walked into a room, your credit profile would be the first impression it makes. You want that first impression to scream, *"I'm reliable, I pay on time, and I mean business."*

Now, here's the MVP of your business identity: the D-U-N-S Number. Sounds fancy, right? It's actually just nine digits, but these nine digits carry some serious weight. Imagine a Social Security number, but instead of tracking you personally, it tracks your business's credibility. Got one? Congratulations! You're officially on the map. No D-U-N-S Number? It's like showing up to a party and realizing the bouncer doesn't even know you exist.

So why is this number such a big deal? Well, first off, it's recognized worldwide. Any serious lender, supplier, or potential partner can look up your business by that number and instantly get a snapshot of your credibility. It's basically your business's handshake in the financial world. You could have the slickest pitch, the best product, or the most killer website, but without a D-U-N-S Number, people might hesitate to take you seriously.

Here's a little secret: you don't need to pay a dime to get one. That's right, Dun & Bradstreet issues D-U-N-S Numbers for free. Some services will try to charge you, but don't fall for it. It's one of those "why pay when it's free?" situations.

Getting your D-U-N-S Number also sets the stage for everything else in your credit profile. Once you have it, you can start building your reputation with the big credit agencies, track how people see your business financially, and even start planning how to score higher when lenders come knocking. It's like planting a tree; the sooner you plant, the sooner it grows strong and shady enough to protect you when things get tricky.

And here's another cool thing: even if your business is brand new, having a D-U-N-S Number shows people you're serious. It says, *"I'm here, I'm organized, and I plan to play the long game."* That's huge, especially when you're trying to get favorable payment terms, open credit lines, or land big contracts.

So yeah, in short: your D-U-N-S Number is small, simple, and free, but it's a total game-changer. Think of it as the foundation of your business credit house. Nail this, and the rest of your credit profile is way easier to build. Skip it, and you're basically trying to build a skyscraper on sand.

Setting Up Your Credit Profiles with Major Agencies

Getting your D-U-N-S Number is just the tip of the iceberg. The next move? Making sure the big credit agencies know your business exists, and trust me, they're paying attention. Think of this like creating your online profile, but for the finance world. You want it clean, accurate, and impressive because everyone from lenders to suppliers is going to peek at it before they make decisions about your business.

The big three agencies you need to know are Dun & Bradstreet (D&B), Experian Business, and Equifax Business. Each one is like a gatekeeper, tracking your business's financial behavior, reporting it, and assigning scores that others rely on. The good news? Signing up is straightforward if you know what info they want. The tricky part is ensuring that your details are correct and optimized, as even minor mistakes can damage your credibility.

Let's start with Dun & Bradstreet. Since you already have a D-U-N-S Number, you're halfway there. Your next move is to claim your business profile on their website. Make sure every detail is accurate, legal business name, address, phone number, and the owner's info. D&B also wants to know about your business structure and the type of industry you operate in. Don't just guess; these things affect how your score is calculated. A clean, complete profile makes you look professional and trustworthy. Pro tip: You can add payment history, trade references, and even a brief description of your business. Every little bit of detail helps.

Next up, Experian Business. Setting up here is also free, but they focus a lot on your payment behavior and financial history. They want to see if you pay invoices on time, how much debt you carry, and whether you've had any collection activity. One thing that trips people up is making sure your business name is exactly the same as it appears on your official documents. Even tiny variations can create duplicate profiles or delays. Experian allows you to check your current business credit score for free, which is a great benefit. You can see where you stand right off the bat.

Then we have Equifax Business, which is often the most detail-oriented of the three. They look at both credit history and public records, like liens or bankruptcies. They also collect information from banks, suppliers, and trade partners. Setting up an account here means entering your basic business info, linking bank accounts if necessary, and confirming your tax ID or EIN. Equifax will start tracking your credit behavior once the profile is live, so accuracy from the start is key.

Now, here's a golden tip across all three agencies: consistency is king. Make sure your business name, address, phone number, and legal structure are identical on every profile. Mismatches can delay scoring, make you appear sloppy, or even create duplicate files, which no lender enjoys navigating.

Another thing, don't just stop at filling in the blanks. Take a moment to optimize your profiles. Add trade references (such as vendors you regularly pay), ensure your business description sounds professional, and keep your contact information current. These details help agencies and potential lenders see your business as reliable and well-managed. It's like dressing your business up for a first impression: neat, polished, and confident.

Finally, remember this isn't a one-and-done task. Profiles need updates as your business grows. Move locations? Change a phone number? Hire new owners or partners? Update it everywhere. The better your profiles look to these agencies, the easier it will be to get favorable lending terms, access higher credit limits, and attract big opportunities.

So, bottom line: claim your profiles, make sure every detail is accurate, optimize where you can, and keep them updated. Do that, and you're not just on the map, you're on it with a business card that says "I'm trustworthy, I'm organized, and I mean business."

Understanding Scoring and Hidden Factors

Now that your business is officially on the radar of the major credit agencies, it's time to talk about something that can make or break your financial game: how your business credit score is calculated. And trust me, this isn't just a boring number; it's the secret sauce that lenders, suppliers, and partners use to decide whether to trust you with money or opportunities.

Business credit scores are a bit like report cards, but instead of grading your math skills, they grade your financial behavior and reliability. Agencies look at a mix of things: payment history, debt levels, public records, credit utilization, and more. Basically, they're trying to answer one question: *"If this business needed credit tomorrow, how likely is it to pay back on time?"*

One of the first things you'll notice is that payment behavior carries a ton of weight. Paying invoices late, missing deadlines, or having collections can seriously tank your score. Even a single late payment can ripple through your profile, making lenders cautious. On the flip side, consistently paying bills on time or early gives you a strong reputation. Think of it like your business sending a message: *"I keep my promises, and I play fair."*

Next up is credit utilization, which is all about how much of your available credit you're actually using. Maxing out credit lines isn't just stressful; it signals risk. Using a smaller portion of your available credit and paying it off regularly shows that you manage resources wisely. It's the financial equivalent of showing restraint in a shopping spree: responsible, reliable, and trustworthy.

But here's where it gets interesting: there are hidden factors that most businesses don't even know about, and understanding these can give you a serious advantage. For example, some agencies consider business age and stability. A company that's been operating for years with a clean financial record is seen as more dependable than a brand-new business, even if both pay bills on time. So while you can't magically make your business older, keeping meticulous records and demonstrating consistent activity helps.

Another consideration that is often overlooked is trade references and supplier relationships. If you have a relationship with vendors who report payments to the credit agencies, that relationship can add to your score... it is pretty much another reputation endorsement from other organizations that says *"yeah, this company is official and pays properly"*.

Here is a little pro tip for you: it pays to watch the trends in your own credit report to identify opportunities for improvement. For example, if an agency identifies high utilization or late payments, you could change your spending habits or pay down your debt faster to increase your credit score. It is similar to being aware that your gas gauge is running low and refueling before you stall on the highway - you just avoid problems before they exacerbate.

Lastly, some agencies also consider legal filings and public records when determining your overall risk. Liens, judgments, or bankruptcies are sure-fire problems, whereas not having any of these issues to begin with adds weight to your standing. This is why it is so important to know what is publicly available about your business and proactively deal with anything that may be less than ideal.

The key takeaway? Scores aren't static; they reflect your actions. Pay attention to how you handle bills, credit, and relationships with partners. Make strategic moves that boost stability and reliability, and you'll notice your score climbing over time. Better scores aren't just numbers; they're tickets to better lending options, higher credit limits, and serious credibility in your industry.

Once you understand scoring and hidden factors, you're no longer guessing; you're playing the business credit game with strategy, not luck. And trust me, once you master this, lenders will start seeing your business in a whole new light: capable, reliable, and ready for opportunities.

Monitoring and Maintaining a Strong Credit Profile

Your business credit profile doesn't sleep. Every invoice, payment, and line of credit leaves a mark, and knowing the score is how you stay ahead. Some actions score points, others can cost you, and the difference between a strong profile and a shaky one is how closely you keep an eye on it.

The first move is checking your credit reports regularly. Even if you're doing everything right, errors happen, an outdated address, a misreported payment, or even a duplicate profile can sneak in. Catching these early is like fixing a tiny leak before it floods the whole system. Make it a habit to review your reports monthly or quarterly so you're never caught off guard.

Next up: automation is a lifesaver. You don't need to babysit every update. Plenty of tools can alert you the moment a change occurs, a new trade line, a shift in your score, or even a public record filing. Think of it as a personal assistant quietly watching your back and alerting you when something needs attention. Many of these alerts are free, and they save a ton of time and stress.

Consistency is another game-changer. Your business name, address, and ownership info should match exactly across all reports. Even small differences, like "Inc." versus "Incorporated", can create duplicate files or slow down how your score is calculated. Clean, uniform information tells lenders and agencies that you're organized, reliable, and on top of things.

Your payment habits remain the backbone of a strong profile. Continue to pay bills on time, avoid maxing out credit lines, and closely monitor your overall debt. Using credit strategically, borrowing when necessary but not overextending, sends a signal that your business is responsible and ready to handle growth.

Relationships matter too. Vendors and suppliers who report payments to credit agencies are like allies vouching for your reliability. Paying on time is a must, but fostering positive relationships and making sure those payments are reported can give your profile a noticeable boost.

Lastly, think in terms of the long game. Just like a credit profile is not built in a few days, nor is a strong reputation. Think of it as a living system: nurtured, monitored, re-evaluated. Updated anytime the business changes location, initial partners, or any other legal changes. Ultimately, the little habits compounded over time create a healthy profile of respectability where closing higher limits, better lending rates, and larger opportunities become possible.

The bottom line? Monitoring and maintaining your credit profile is not just a reasonable consideration; it's a requirement. It requires strategy and effort, but it's no more difficult than that. Stay aware, stay ahead of issues, and make the right financial decisions. Your credit profile will tell a compelling story for your business: trustworthy, capable, and reliable.

Chapter 05: Net 30 Vendors: Your First Step

Understanding Net 30 Terms – Your First Step Toward Building Business Credit

If you've never heard of business credit before, then "Net 30" might seem like some weird phrase that only corporate finance fanatics know about. But in truth, it is easier to understand than you may think, and it is far less scary than it appears. "Net 30" is really just a vendor's way of saying, "Buy now, pay later, with the payment due in 30 days." With "Net 30", you can order supplies, equipment, etc., for your business, and run the 30-day timer before you owe any cash.

You do not pay cash up front; instead, you have 30 full days to pay. Miss that deadline, and you may be paying for late fees, interest, or a ding on your business credit. If you pay on time, you are looking good in the eyes of potential lenders and credit bureaus because you are demonstrating that your business can be responsible.

Why does this matter? Well, think of Net 30 terms as training wheels for your business credit. You're not borrowing huge sums from a bank yet. You're starting small, making manageable payments, and building a record of reliability. Each timely payment is like a tiny victory badge that says, *"Hey, this business knows how to handle its money."* And lenders notice. That positive history can open doors to bigger lines of credit, better financing options, and even improved vendor relationships down the line.

Net 30 is also flexible. You can use it for essentials in your day-to-day operation, such as office supplies, packaging, or small inventory, while not locking up your cash flow. Cash flow is king for a new business owner, and Net 30 helps you keep more of your assets working for you instead of being in someone else's account. Just remember, it is about using it strategically, starting with one or two accounts and making on-time payments as a habit, and you will see your credit profile start to take shape.

Here is the best part: not only do Net 30 vendors report your payments to the business credit bureaus, but they also help you learn discipline. You will learn how to track invoices, manage payment schedules, and develop a plan for your cash flow in a way that will more efficiently navigate your finances. These small steps will quickly become a habit - before you know it, you are fielding much larger financial maneuvers with the same ability.

Why Net 30 Vendors Are the Backbone of Business Credit

Think of Net 30 vendors as the unsung heroes of your business credit journey. They're the ones quietly keeping score of your financial reliability, long before any bank or big lender even thinks about giving you a line of credit. Unlike personal credit, which is often tied to your Social Security number and personal history, business credit lives in its own world. And in that world, vendors are the referees; they report how you handle payments, and those reports build the narrative of your business's financial health.

Every time you pay a vendor on time, it's like earning points toward your credibility. Vendors report these payments to business credit bureaus, which in turn creates a track record showing that your company can manage its obligations responsibly. The more consistent your payments, the stronger your reputation becomes. Large lenders, such as banks and financing companies, review these histories before extending larger opportunities. They want proof that you're trustworthy, and nothing speaks louder than a string of well-managed Net 30 accounts.

What makes vendors even more critical is that they're often the first entities willing to extend credit to a new business. Banks typically require a few years of operational history, revenue records, or collateral. Vendors, however, are willing to give you a chance on smaller, manageable accounts. That's why these accounts are foundational; they give you a safe playground to show that your business can be financially responsible, without risking huge sums of money.

Additionally, working with Net 30 vendors teaches you practical financial habits. You'll get accustomed to reading invoices carefully, reconciling statements, and planning cash flow in advance. These are not just good practices; they're signals to the market that your business is stable and reliable. Over time, as you accumulate a history of timely payments with multiple vendors, your business develops a kind of credibility "score" that bigger financial institutions take seriously.

In short, Net 30 vendors are more than just suppliers; they're your credibility architects. They help you build a track record that positions your business for larger credit lines, favorable financing terms, and a strong professional reputation. The better you work with them, the more they help you grow your financial foundation, turning small credit opportunities into big business advantages.

Finding the Best Starter Vendors That Report and Picking the Right Ones

Not all Net 30 vendors are created equal, and this is where strategy comes in. Some vendors are picky, some are easygoing, and some don't even report your payments to the credit bureaus, which means paying them on time does nothing for your business credit. The trick is to find those golden starter vendors that do report and are friendly to newcomers. These are the accounts that can actually help your business build a credible, visible history without making you jump through unnecessary hoops.

When choosing vendors, you want a mix of reliability, accessibility, and reporting power. Vendors like Quill, Uline, and Grainger are popular choices because they have established systems for reporting payments to major business credit bureaus. That's like having a trusted referee in the game of building credit; they make sure every successful payment gets recorded. But don't ignore the lesser-known vendors. Sometimes, smaller suppliers are more flexible and easier to get approved for, giving you a low-risk way to start stacking positive accounts.

Selection isn't just about who reports; it's also about what fits your business. Ask yourself: What do I actually need for operations? Do I need office supplies, packaging materials, or tools? There's no point in opening an account for the sake of credit if you won't use it responsibly. Start with vendors whose products or services your business truly requires. That way, every purchase is purposeful, every payment on time, and every account contributes to your credit history.

Another smart move is to diversify your vendors. Don't put all your eggs in one basket. A mix of product types and reporting vendors shows that your business can manage multiple accounts simultaneously. Lenders and credit bureaus notice this, and it signals that your company is organized, responsible, and capable of handling growth.

Finally, be methodical in your applications. Some vendors might require basic business info, tax IDs, or a business bank account. Take the time to fill everything out correctly; errors or incomplete applications can slow your progress. Once approved, keep track of each account, know your payment deadlines, and gradually expand. By choosing the right starter vendors and managing them strategically, you're creating a solid foundation for your business credit, one smart account at a time.

A Complete List of Verified Net 30 Vendors – Big Names and Hidden Gems

Once you understand what Net 30 is and why vendors matter, the next step is knowing *who* to work with. Luckily, there are a handful of trusted vendors that consistently report payments to business credit bureaus. Think of these as your VIP list, the ones that can actually move the needle on your credit profile. Big names like Quill, Uline, and Grainger are household staples in the business credit world. They're reliable, widely recognized, and excellent for establishing a strong payment history. Quill is perfect for office supplies, Uline covers packaging and shipping needs, and Grainger handles tools and industrial equipment. Starting with these ensures your first trade lines are solid and reported properly.

But here's the secret: you don't have to stick only to the big players. There's a whole world of lesser-known vendors who are easier to get approved with, often requiring less stringent business history or lower initial orders. These vendors are especially useful if you're just starting out and want to avoid the stress of waiting for approvals or stretching your finances too thin. Combining a few of these smaller vendors with one or two of the big names gives your business both credibility and flexibility.

It's also smart to consider the types of products you're ordering. Some vendors specialize in office needs, some in marketing materials, and others in equipment or tools. Pick vendors whose products you'll actually use; this way, every order is practical, and your payments feel natural instead of forced. Over time, these accounts accumulate, showing a pattern of responsible behavior that lenders and credit bureaus love to see.

In short, having a curated list of Net 30 vendors, mixing the big, recognizable names with some easier-to-get accounts, sets you up for success. You're not just collecting vendors randomly; you're building a network of accounts that actively contribute to your credit profile, teaching financial responsibility, and giving you a practical, low-risk way to grow your business credit from the ground up.

Using Vendor Accounts Strategically to Build Credit Without Overstretching

Opening Net 30 accounts is just the start; the real game is how you use them wisely. You don't want to pile up orders just for the sake of credit, because that can quickly turn into cash-flow headaches or excess inventory that's hard to manage. The goal is to leverage these accounts to grow your credit profile *intelligently*, without putting your business at financial risk.

Think of it like training for a marathon. You wouldn't sprint your first mile; you'd start slow, pace yourself, and gradually increase the distance. With vendor accounts, the same principle applies. Start with one or two accounts, make smaller, manageable purchases, and pay them on time. Each completed cycle strengthens your credit history and gives you confidence to handle more significant accounts later.

The strategy also involves prioritizing accounts based on reporting impact. Not every vendor reports to every credit bureau, and not all accounts have the same weight in building a solid credit profile. By focusing on vendors that consistently report and have an influence on your overall business score, you get the most bang for your buck. It's less about how much you spend and more about showing a reliable pattern of responsible payment.

Another key part of this strategy is keeping track of due dates and payment schedules. A simple spreadsheet or accounting software can help you visualize upcoming payments, so you never miss a deadline. Missed or late payments don't just cost money; they can undo the progress you've carefully built. By keeping a disciplined approach, you maintain momentum without risking financial stress.

Finally, this strategy is about balance. You want to expand your credit footprint steadily, not recklessly. By using vendor accounts in a controlled, strategic way, you're building a strong, measurable history that lenders and other vendors can trust. Over time, this approach transforms small, routine orders into a powerful foundation for higher credit limits, better financing, and overall business growth.

How to Place Orders Like a Credit-Building Pro (Without Losing Your Mind or Money)

So, you've got your Net 30 accounts, congrats! But don't go crazy thinking you need to buy everything in sight. The real trick is knowing how to use them smartly so your credit grows and your wallet doesn't cry.

Start small. Yeah, that fancy office chair or bulk pack of pens can wait. Make a few manageable purchases first. It's like flexing your credit muscles. Start with light weights, not the heaviest dumbbells in the gym. Each on-time payment is basically a high-five from the credit bureaus.

Timing is everything. Don't hit all your accounts on the same day; it's like trying to eat a 12-course meal in one sitting. Spread out your orders so your activity looks natural and steady. This way, your cash flow doesn't scream, *"HELP, I SPENT IT ALL!"*

Buy stuff you actually need. No pointless splurges. Every purchase should make sense for your business. It keeps your expenses real, your inventory useful, and your accounting way less of a nightmare. Vendors like seeing purposeful transactions; it makes them think, "Yep, this business knows what it's doing."

Finally, don't max out your limits. Using a little bit of credit and paying it off shows discipline. Over time, vendors will trust you more and maybe even raise your limits. Boom, you just leveled up your credit game without breaking the bank.

In short: pace yourself, buy smart, and keep it real. Your credit grows, your cash stays intact, and you look like a pro, without any of the chaos.

Managing Your Net 30 Accounts Without Stressing Out

So, you've got your accounts, you're making orders, and your credit is slowly leveling up, but now comes the part most people trip over: actually managing them. Don't worry, it's not rocket science. It's more like juggling, just with money instead of flaming torches.

First things first: keep a list. Whether it's a spreadsheet, an app, or a sticky note on your fridge (hey, whatever works), know which accounts you have, what you owe, and when payments are due. Missing a due date isn't just embarrassing; it can hurt your credit progress, and nobody wants that.

Next, treat these accounts like little mini-bosses. Pay attention to their rules, due dates, and any fees. Some vendors are super chill, but others can be strict. Showing that you respect their system earns you trust, and trust is the secret sauce for long-term credit growth.

Also, don't overcomplicate things. You don't need a massive inventory of stuff you'll never use just to "look active." Make meaningful purchases that actually support your business. That way, payments are easy, predictable, and you're not drowning in random office supplies.

Finally, stay consistent. Set reminders, schedule payments if you can, and check your accounts regularly. The key isn't flashiness; it's reliability. A smooth, steady track record makes your business look solid to lenders, credit bureaus, and even the vendors themselves.

Bottom line: managing your Net 30 accounts isn't about doing everything at once; it's about keeping it organized, simple, and consistent. Do that, and your business credit will thank you.

Getting Your Payment Timing and Account Habits Right

Alright, let's get real, payment timing is everything. You can have all the best vendors, rock-solid orders, and perfectly managed accounts, but if your payments are late, all that effort doesn't mean much. Business credit isn't just about having accounts; it's about proving you can handle them responsibly, like a pro who knows what they're doing.

The key trick? Keep your due dates front and center. Set calendar alerts, phone reminders, or automatic payments if possible. Think of it as giving yourself a gentle nudge instead of letting the bills sneak up on you. Missing a date isn't just a little oops; it can delay reporting, hurt your credit, and make your life way more stressful.

Another habit to build: pay the full balance when you can. Partial payments are fine sometimes, but full, on-time payments show lenders and credit bureaus that your business isn't just surviving, it's thriving. This is the kind of behavior that makes you look responsible, reliable, and ready for bigger opportunities.

Also, get into a rhythm with your vendors. Check your invoices, track what's coming due, and mark your calendar with recurring orders and payments. Treat your Net 30 accounts like a routine, not a surprise challenge every month. When it becomes second nature, you'll be amazed at how easy building a strong credit profile feels.

In short: pay on time, pay smart, and be consistent. Nail the timing, and you're not just keeping vendors happy, you're building a reputation that opens doors for more credit, better terms, and serious business growth.

Why Paying on Time Makes You Look Like a Rockstar (and a Responsible Business Owner)

Let's cut to the chase: paying your Net 30 bills on time isn't just about avoiding late fees, it's about showing the world your business knows how to handle its money. Lenders, vendors, and credit bureaus are basically keeping a scoreboard, and every on-time payment is a point in your favor. Miss a payment, and that scoreboard takes a hit.

Think of it this way: paying late is like showing up to a job interview in pajamas; it leaves a bad impression, even if everything else is perfect. Paying on time, on the other hand, is like showing up sharp, confident, and ready to impress. That consistency builds trust and credibility, which is exactly what your business needs to grow.

Another cool thing? On-time payments help your credit score climb steadily. Every month you make timely payments adds to a track record that says, *"This business knows what it's doing."* And guess what? The better your score, the easier it gets to snag bigger credit lines, better vendor terms, and even funding opportunities that once seemed out of reach.

It's not just about numbers, either; it's about reputation. Vendors remember businesses that pay on time. They're more likely to offer higher limits, special deals, or even say yes to your orders faster. Basically, paying on time makes you the business equivalent of a superstar client.

So, bottom line: don't treat your Net 30 payments like an afterthought. Set reminders, plan your cash flow, and pay every invoice on time. It's simple, but it's one of the most powerful things you can do for your credit, your reputation, and your business's future.

Setting Yourself Up for Bigger Wins with Net 30 Accounts

Now that you've got the hang of Net 30 vendors, it's time to think bigger. These accounts aren't just small credit tools; they're the building blocks for future opportunities. By handling them smartly, you're basically laying down the first layer of a financial empire for your business.

When your payments are solid, your accounts are well-managed, and your credit history is clean, lenders start seeing you as more than just a new business; they see you as a reliable partner. That opens doors to larger credit lines, better financing options, and even exclusive vendor deals that other businesses might only dream about.

Another perk? Confidence. Managing Net 30 accounts successfully teaches you how to juggle multiple financial responsibilities without sweating bullets. You'll develop habits for budgeting, scheduling payments, and making smart purchasing decisions that pay off down the line. These habits translate directly into bigger financial moves, like securing loans, investing in inventory, or scaling operations.

Think of it this way: each well-managed account is like a brick in your business credit foundation. Alone, it's helpful, but together, they create a strong structure that supports bigger, more ambitious goals. Mastering Net 30 accounts now means when it's time to go for larger lines of credit, business loans, or partnerships, you're not scrambling; you're ready.

Bottom line: treat your Net 30 accounts as more than just small orders. Handle them wisely, learn from them, and let them set the stage for bigger, smarter financial moves in the future. Your business growth and credit potential depend on it, and the earlier you nail this, the faster you can reach those next-level opportunities.

Chapter 06: Building Tier 2 And Tier 3 Credit

From Net 30 Accounts to Scalable Credit

Starting a business is kind of like learning how to ride a bike. At first, you don't just hop on a big mountain bike and race down a hill; you start with training wheels. That's exactly what Net 30 vendor accounts are for your business.

When you're new to the world of business credit, vendors like Quill, Uline, and Granger give you your first shot at proving you can handle financial responsibility. They'll let you order supplies, send you an invoice, and expect payment in 30 days. Simple deal, right? But here's the magic: when you pay those invoices *on time*, it doesn't just keep the lights on; it starts leaving footprints in the credit world.

Think of every payment as a small signal to the business credit bureaus:

"Hey, this company is trustworthy. They pay their bills."

Over a few months, those small signals start to stack up into an actual credit profile. And while it might not feel like much, you're just buying paper, pens, or cleaning supplies, it's like building the foundation of a house. Without that solid base, nothing bigger can stand on top.

The important thing to remember? Net 30 accounts are not about what you're buying; they're about what you're providing. You're showing lenders, suppliers, and future partners that your business can be counted on. That reliability is your golden ticket to bigger opportunities later.

So yes, ordering printer paper and paying it off on time may feel boring... but behind the scenes, it's the first chapter in your business credit story. And every great story needs a strong beginning.

The Path to Tier 2 and Tier 3 Credit

So, you've got your training wheels on. You've been paying off those Net 30 invoices, building a little reputation with the credit bureaus, and now you're ready to take the next step. This is where most new business owners get excited, and also where a lot of them get stuck. Because while Net 30 accounts are a great starting point, they only get you so far. It's kind of like flexing with a learner's driving permit; you're on the road, but nobody's handing you the keys to a Ferrari yet.

That's where Tier 2 credit comes into play. Think of Tier 2 as your first upgrade, the moment you take the training wheels off and start riding on your own. At this stage, you're no longer just buying paperclips and cleaning supplies. Instead, you're getting access to store cards, gas cards, and even small fleet accounts. These give you way more flexibility because now you can buy the stuff that actually grows your business, not just keeps it running day-to-day.

But the credit world wants proof that you're ready for that kind of trust. To qualify for Tier 2, your business usually needs:

- At least 3 to 5 Net 30 accounts reporting to the bureaus.
- A Paydex score of 70 or higher (translation: you've been paying on time, maybe even early).
- A business that's properly listed with all the big guys, Dun & Bradstreet, Experian, and Equifax.
- And at least a few months of clean payment history.

Once you've got those ducks in a row, doors start opening. Suddenly, you can apply for accounts like Amazon Business, Office Depot, Sam's Club, BP, Chevron, and more. Some might still ask for a personal guarantee, but many won't. If you've built your profile right, your business credit will be enough to get approval.

Now, once you've mastered Tier 2, you're not done. Nope, there's another level. Tier 3 credit is where things start to get really interesting. These accounts don't just prove you can handle responsibility; they show lenders that your business is maturing into a real player. Tier 3 comes with higher limits, better terms, and a lot more freedom in how you spend.

The requirements are a bit steeper. Usually, you'll need:

- Around 5 to 8 trade lines are reporting.

- 6 to 12 months of clean history (no late payments, no funny business).
- Strong scores across the board, not just Paydex, but also Experian and Equifax ratings.

With that kind of profile, you unlock access to cards and accounts from places like Costco Business, Home Depot, Best Buy for Business, advanced fleet cards, American Express, Walmart Business, and more. These aren't little starter accounts anymore; these are heavy hitters that can move the needle for your business.

Think of it this way: Net 30 accounts get you on the board, Tier 2 gets you in the game, but Tier 3? That's when you finally start playing in the big leagues. Bigger limits, broader flexibility, and a whole lot more credibility in the eyes of banks and lenders.

And the best part? You earned it. You proved you could handle the basics, you showed consistency, and now you've got the kind of credit that can actually help your business grow, not just survive.

Why Store, Gas & Fleet Cards Matter

Alright, let's be honest, when you hear "store card" or "gas card," it doesn't exactly scream exciting, right? Most people imagine those little retail credit cards that pushy cashiers try to sell you at checkout. But in the world of business credit? These cards are a whole different ball game. They're not just shiny plastic; they're strategic tools that can literally fuel your business (pun intended).

Let's start with store cards. These aren't limited to office supplies anymore. With the right store account, you can grab laptops, printers, furniture, and even the software that keeps your business running smoothly. And here's the kicker: a lot of these store cards report to multiple credit bureaus. That means every time you swipe and pay responsibly, your business credit profile is getting stronger and stronger across the board. It's like free PR for your company's reputation.

And here's where it gets fun, limits. Unlike vendor accounts, store cards often start with higher spending power, and if you keep proving yourself, those limits grow. Imagine starting with a $2,000 card, and within a year, that same account is offering you $15,000. That kind of room gives you real leverage to make bigger moves without draining your cash flow. One small agency did exactly that: they started off with a simple Amazon Business card, bought laptops for their team, paid it down fast, and less than a year later, they were celebrating a $20,000 line of credit from a bank. The store card was their stepping stone.

Now, let's talk gas and fleet cards. These are the unsung heroes, especially if your business has anything to do with transportation, delivery services, logistics, sales reps driving across the state, or even a landscaping crew with a few trucks. Gas is one of those expenses you *know* is going to hit every single month. So why not make it work for you?

With a fleet card, you're not just paying for fuel; you're also tracking mileage, employee spending, and even spotting waste or inefficiencies. Plus, a lot of these cards come with sweet perks like rebates, discounts, or points. For a company burning through hundreds (or thousands) of dollars in gas each month, that's money back in your pocket. And every swipe is another positive mark on your credit profile.

Take this real-world style example: a small landscaping company with three trucks. Before fleet cards, they were just handing out cash or personal debit cards for gas. Messy, hard to track, and zero impact on business credit. After switching to fleet cards, not only did they save hundreds each month with fuel discounts, but their organized payment history also gave their business credit score a serious boost. Within a year, they were approved for financing that allowed them to buy a fourth truck, something that never would've happened if they were still paying cash at the pump.

Store, gas, and fleet cards aren't just "credit cards." They're proof that your business can handle real-world, recurring expenses like a pro. They widen your buying power, build your reputation with lenders, and, when used strategically, open doors to bigger and better funding. Think of them as the bridge between surviving and thriving.

Best Practices, Pitfalls & Long-Term Vision

By the time you're juggling Net 30s, store cards, and maybe even a fleet card or two, it's tempting to think, *"Cool, I've got this credit thing figured out."* But here's the truth: business credit is a bit like fitness. It's not just about starting strong; it's about staying consistent. One slip, one late payment, one maxed-out account, and all that hard work can come crashing down.

Let's start with the best practices that separate the pros from the amateurs:

- **Pay early, not just on time.** Credit bureaus love seeing early payments. It's like showing up to a meeting 10 minutes early; you instantly look more reliable.
- **Keep your balances light.** If you've got a $5,000 limit, don't flirt with $4,800 in charges. Staying under 30% shows you're in control, not desperate.
- **Stay organized.** Whether it's autopay, a Google calendar reminder, or bookkeeping software like QuickBooks, find a system that keeps due dates from sneaking up on you.

- **Be picky.** Don't apply for every shiny new account you see. Each inquiry leaves a mark, and too many, too fast, make you look risky.

Now, onto the red flags, the stuff that can tank your credibility faster than you'd expect:

- Applying everywhere like you're speed-dating credit companies.
- Carrying high balances for months on end (lenders start sweating when they see that).
- Missing a single due date, it sounds dramatic, but one late payment can drop your score like a rock.
- Ignoring your reports. Imagine applying for a big loan and finding out there's an error dragging down your score. If you're not checking, you'd never know.

Business credit is more than just access to money. It's about setting up your business for the long game. When you build a strong profile, you're not just opening doors for the next six months; you're creating a foundation your company can stand on for years.

Think about it like this: your personal credit score impacts only you. But your business credit profile can outlive you. Done right, it separates your personal finances from your company's, protects your personal credit, and creates a system your business, and even your kids, can inherit. Imagine your son or daughter stepping into the family business one day. Instead of starting from zero, they walk into a company with a credit history, a reputation, and the ability to secure funding without breaking a sweat. That's real generational wealth.

At the end of the day, business credit isn't about chasing cards or bragging about high limits. It's about using credit strategically, like a tool, not a toy. If you keep your habits sharp, avoid the traps, and think bigger than just today's expenses, your credit profile stops being a fragile beginner's resume and starts becoming a powerful portfolio that banks, lenders, and investors respect.

And that, right there, is the difference between a business that struggles to survive and one that's built to thrive for decades.

Chapter 07: Bank Loans And Business Credit Cards

Introduction: Why Funding Matters for Small Businesses

Starting a business usually begins with excitement, late nights, and a lot of dreaming. What it rarely begins with is a pile of cash waiting to be spent. Most new owners open their doors with whatever they can scrape together. Savings. A small personal loan. Maybe a family member who's willing to chip in. It works for a little while, but it doesn't stretch far.

Opening week? You might be able to buy supplies and cover rent. Month two? Suddenly, you're wondering how to pay for marketing, a new employee, or even replacing a broken piece of equipment. That's when reality sinks in: running a business takes more money than you first imagined.

The first stage of funding is usually personal. You rely on your own credit cards, your own bank account, your own name. There's nothing wrong with that, but personal money only takes you so far. At some point, you'll want to step into bigger shoes: real business credit, loans, or lines of funding from banks and lenders who don't just see you as an individual but as a company worth backing.

That shift is huge. It's the difference between patching things together month by month and actually planning ahead. With professional funding, you can grow faster, take bigger opportunities, and stop worrying about whether tomorrow's deposits will cover today's bills.

But here's the challenge. Lenders don't hand out money because you've worked hard or because you "believe in your dream." They want proof. They want structure. They want to know your business is stable, organized, and capable of paying them back without drama.

Every bank, credit union, or online lender will look at the same four areas before deciding on your application: your legal setup, your credit history, your cash flow, and the story of your business. This chapter is going to break those down piece by piece, so you'll know exactly what they're checking for and how to prepare.

And it won't stop there. We'll also walk through how to start small, like using secured credit cards, then move up to unsecured cards, business credit lines, and eventually bank or SBA loans. You'll see how to package yourself so you don't just apply for money, you actually get approved.

By the time you're done with this chapter, you'll have a clear picture of what lenders want, how to give it to them, and how to turn that approval into the kind of funding that actually grows your business.

The Four Core Things Every Lender Looks For

When you walk into a bank, or apply online for that matter, the person reviewing your file isn't judging whether your idea is "cool" or whether your logo looks sharp. They're asking four big questions. If you can check all four boxes, you're in a strong position to get approved. If you're weak in even one, that's often where the denial happens.

Legal and Business Setup

The first thing a lender looks at is whether you're actually a *real* business. Not real as in "you have customers," but real on paper. That means proper structure and consistent documents.

- **Business structure:** Are you a sole proprietor, LLC, or S-corp? Lenders prefer seeing an LLC or corporation because it shows separation between you and your business. A sole proprietor might still get small funding, but big banks like it.
- **EIN:** This is your Employer Identification Number from the IRS. Think of it like a social security number for your business. Without it, lenders can't even start the process.
- **Business licenses/permits:** Depending on your industry, you may need a local license, state registration, or specific certifications. Missing these is an easy red flag.
- **Consistency:** Your LLC papers say "Sarah's Cakes LLC," but your bank account says "Sarah's Bakery"? Lender's notice. All addresses, names, and documents need to match.

Mini Case Study: Mark, a landscaper, applied for a $20,000 credit line. He had the sales and the credit score, but his bank account was still in his personal name while his LLC paperwork showed a business name. The bank flagged it as "inconsistent paperwork" and denied him. Once he cleaned it up, new account, consistent documents, he got approved on his second try.

Credit History

In the early days, your business has no credit history. So, guess whose credit matters? Yours.

- **Personal credit:** Most lenders want to see a score of at least 580–640 for entry-level funding. Mid-level business cards usually require 650–680. The best cards and bank loans often want 700+.
- **Payment history:** More important than huge limits is a clean record of paying on time. Even one missed payment can raise eyebrows.
- **Transition to business credit:** As you build, lenders eventually start checking Dun & Bradstreet, Experian Business, and Equifax Business. These reports track your company's payment history separate from your personal credit.

Pro Tip: Before applying, pull your own credit report. Fix mistakes, pay down high balances, and avoid applying for anything if your score is too low. Even paying off a small credit card can bump you up a tier.

Cash Flow and Sales

Banks don't just want to see revenue; they want to see *steady revenue.*

- **Consistency over spikes:** $10,000 one month and $0 the next looks unstable. $3,000 every month looks safer.
- **Proof:** They'll ask for bank statements, tax returns, or accounting records. Lenders want to see deposits hitting your account regularly.
- **Tools:** Software like QuickBooks or Wave can help you keep clean records, which lenders love.

Example: Compare two bank statements.

- **Weak statement:** $5,000 deposit in March, nothing in April, $7,000 in May.
- **Strong statement:** $3,500 in March, $3,800 in April, $4,100 in May.

Guess which business looks healthier? The second one, even though the total is smaller.

Your Business Story

Numbers matter, but they don't tell the whole story. Lenders want to know what you *do*, who you serve, and where you're headed.

- **Clarity:** Can you explain your business in 2–3 sentences without confusing anyone?
- **Vision:** Do you have a clear plan for growth? Even modest plans are fine; what matters is direction.
- **Customers:** Lenders like knowing who your market is. "We sell to homeowners in our county" sounds stronger than "We sell to anyone, anywhere."

Quick Exercise: Try building a 30-second pitch for funding.

- **Weak version:** "I run a bakery and just need money to grow."
- **Strong version:** "I own Sarah's Cakes, a bakery serving our local community. We've doubled sales in the last year and want to add new equipment to handle catering orders. With a $25,000 credit line, we'll increase capacity by 40% and take on larger clients."

That's the kind of story that makes a lender think: This person knows where they're going, and they have a plan to use our money wisely.

The Path: From Secured Cards to Major Bank Lines

Every business owner dreams of swiping a shiny business credit card with a five-figure limit. But the truth? Almost nobody starts there. The path to those big credit lines usually begins with something much less glamorous: a secured card. It might feel small, even frustrating at first, but it's the exact stepping stone that gets you to the real money.

A. Secured Credit Cards: The First Step

A secured card works like training wheels. You put down a deposit, usually somewhere between $300 and $1,000, and that deposit becomes your limit. So if you hand over $500, congratulations, you now have a card with a $500 limit. It's not exciting, but it's safe for the bank and a chance for you to prove yourself.

Most people start with banks like Wells Fargo or Bank of America, since they both offer solid secured options.

The rules are simple:

- Pay on time.
- Keep your balance low (under 30% of your limit).
- Stick with it for 6 to 12 months.

Do that, and you're showing lenders the exact behavior they want to see.

Example: Sarah, the bakery owner, started with a $500 secured card. She treated it like gold, never missed a payment, and never carried a balance over $150. After nine months, her bank upgraded her to an unsecured card with a $3,000 limit. That was her first real step toward business-level funding.

Some people move faster than others. If you're consistent and already have halfway decent personal credit, you might "graduate" in six months. If your score is shaky, it might take a year. The key is discipline.

Unsecured Credit Cards: The Graduation

Once you've shown you can handle a secured card, banks are usually willing to trust you with more. This is when you unlock unsecured credit cards, cards where you don't have to put down a deposit.

Unsecured cards typically start around $5,000 limits but can scale up fast. With consistent payments and strong credit, you could jump to $20,000 or even $50,000 over time. Banks love rewarding good behavior.

Popular options here include:

- **Capital One Spark** (great for small businesses starting out).
- **Chase Ink** (solid rewards and higher limits as you grow).
- **American Express Gold or Platinum** (premium options, but they expect strong personal credit).

Visual idea: Imagine a chart showing the difference:

- Secured card = $500 limit, requires a deposit.
- Unsecured starter = $5,000–$10,000 limit.
- Premium unsecured = $20,000+ limit, no deposit.

That's the climb most businesses follow.

Business Credit Cards and Lines of Credit

Here's where things start feeling real. Business credit cards and credit lines open doors to larger amounts of money, and they're in your business's name, not yours.

The requirements get steeper:

- A personal credit score of 650–680 for mid-level cards.
- At least $25,000 to $100,000 in annual revenue.

Examples:

- Chase Ink Business Preferred.
- Capital One Spark Cash.

Once your revenue passes six figures and your score hits 700+, premium cards open up. That's when you can snag an Amex Business Platinum or other big-limit cards. These often start around $20,000 and can easily stretch higher if your business shows steady cash flow.

Most businesses won't jump straight to Amex Platinum in their first year. It's a ladder, not an elevator. If you know that going in, you won't feel discouraged when your first "real" business card tops out at $7,500. That's part of the process.

Bank & SBA Loans

At the top of the ladder sit bank loans and SBA-backed loans. These are the big players. To qualify, you usually need:

- A personal credit score of 680–700+.
- At least $200,000 in annual revenue.

Traditional banks are strict; they want to see solid numbers and a proven track record. SBA loans (backed by the government) are a little more flexible, but they still want stability. The upside is that SBA loans often come with better terms and lower rates than online lenders.

A lot of business owners hear "SBA loan" and think it's impossible. It's not. It just takes time, paperwork, and patience. If you're steady and organized, this is where you unlock the serious money that fuels expansion.

How to Package Yourself for Approval

So, let's say you've done the groundwork, you've built some credit history, your sales are coming in, and you're ready to knock on the bank's door. Now comes the part that trips a lot of business owners up: packaging yourself.

Think of this like showing up to a job interview. You might be super talented, but if you walk in wearing flip-flops and no resume, you're not getting the gig. Same with lenders. They want to see your numbers, but they also want the whole thing neatly wrapped up in a way that screams, *"This person is serious, responsible, and worth betting on."*

A. Executive Summary

Start with one page, literally. Who you are, what your business does, and why funding matters. That's it. Don't overcomplicate this. Banks don't want a novel; they want a snapshot.

Example:

"I run Sarah's Sweet Spot, a bakery specializing in artisan breads and pastries. In two years, we've grown from selling at farmers' markets to a storefront with steady foot traffic. We're seeking $50,000 to purchase a commercial oven that will increase production capacity by 40% and allow us to take on wholesale accounts."

That tells the lender exactly who you are, what you're doing, and why the money makes sense. Short, clear, professional.

B. Financial Proof

Now comes the meat: your financials. No way around this. You'll need:

- Tax returns.
- Profit and loss statements.

- Bank statements showing consistent deposits.

Lenders aren't necessarily looking for giant profits. What they want is stability. Steady deposits every month look way better than wild spikes.

- Weak example → $20,000 one month, then $500 the next.
- Strong example → $5,000 every month for a year.

Consistency builds trust. If you can back your numbers up with clean records, you're already ahead of half the competition.

C. Business Plan

Forget the 50-page documents you've seen floating around online. Most lenders don't want to read that. What they actually want: a short plan that shows you know where you're headed.

Your plan should cover three things:

- What do you sell?
- Who buys it?
- Where are you going next?

Example: Mark the landscaper, put together a two-page plan showing how adding two new trucks would double the number of houses his crew could service each week. That's clear, realistic, and easy for a lender to understand.

A short, sharp plan will always beat a long, fluffy one.

D. Use of Funds

Finally, tell them exactly what the money's for. This is where a lot of people blow it by being vague. Saying *"We need $50,000 for growth"* doesn't cut it. Growth how? Growth where?

Better example:

"We need $50,000 to buy two commercial ovens. These ovens increase capacity by 40%, letting us serve wholesale clients. That expansion is projected to add $120,000 in annual revenue within 18 months."

That's a clear case: specific purchase, measurable outcome, realistic return.

Banks love this level of detail. It makes them feel safe because they can picture exactly how their money is being used to make more money.

That's the full package: story, numbers, plan, and purpose. Put those pieces together, and instead of being "just another applicant," you look like the business owner who has their act together. And trust me, lenders notice.

Alternatives If Banks Say No

Let's be real, sometimes, no matter how prepared you feel, the bank just isn't ready to take a chance on you yet. That doesn't mean the dream dies. It just means you need to look at other doors. And luckily, there are quite a few of them.

SBA Microloans

Think of these as the "training wheels" of business loans. They're smaller, usually up to $50,000, but easier to get approved for than a big traditional loan. These are backed by the government (through the Small Business Administration), which makes lenders more comfortable handing you the cash.

It's slower paperwork-wise, but if you can wait a little, it's one of the safest ways to get legit funding when the big banks say no.

Online Lenders

When banks move at the speed of a sloth, online lenders are like cheetahs. Companies like Kabbage, BlueVine, or OnDeck can approve you in days, sometimes even hours.

The tradeoff? Interest rates are higher. But if you're in a pinch and need money fast to grab an opportunity, this route works. Just treat it like a short-term fix, not your forever plan.

Merchant Cash Advances (MCAs)

This one comes with a giant caution sign. An MCA gives you money upfront, but instead of a fixed payment plan, they take a cut of your future sales until it's paid back.

Sounds flexible, right? The problem is the fees. They're often sky-high, which means you can get trapped paying way more than you borrowed. MCAs are like junk food, okay, once in a while, but don't build your whole diet on them.

Credit Unions

These smaller, community-based institutions don't get talked about enough. Unlike massive banks, credit unions actually like building relationships. If you've been a loyal member (or become one), they're often more willing to say yes to someone just getting started.

Plus, their rates and fees are usually better. Think of them as the "friendly neighbor" in the lending world.

Quick Pros & Cons Snapshot

Option	Pros	Cons
SBA Microloans	Easier approval, lower rates	Slow process, lots of paperwork
Online Lenders	Fast approvals, flexible amounts	Higher interest, short repayment
Merchant Cash Advance	Quick cash, based on sales	Very expensive, risky long-term
Credit Unions	Relationship-based, lower fees	Smaller amounts, membership needed

If the bank turns you away, don't take it personally. It happens all the time. What matters is knowing these alternatives exist so you can keep moving forward instead of stalling out.

Mistakes That Get You Denied

Getting denied for funding stings. You spend all that time gathering documents, filling out forms, maybe even psyching yourself up for that "yes," and then, boom, it's a rejection letter. The worst part? Many times it's avoidable. Let's break down the most common reasons lenders slam the brakes, so you can dodge them before they trip you up.

1. Applying Without Knowing Your Credit Score

Imagine walking into an exam without checking what subject it's on. That's basically what applying for funding blind is like. Lenders don't just "glance" at your score; it's one of their first filters.

I once heard about a guy who was confident his score was "pretty good." Turns out it was 560. Not terrible for a personal card, but way too low for the business funding he was shooting for. Denied instantly.

Before you even apply, check your personal and business credit. Clean up errors, pay down balances, and know where you stand. Walking in prepared puts you miles ahead.

2. Maxing Out Your Accounts

Lenders want to see breathing room in your finances. If every credit card is at 95% usage and your bank account dips to $12 before payday, that's a red flag.

Think of it this way: if you're already juggling flaming torches, why would a lender hand you another one? Keeping your balances under 30% of your limits shows discipline and lowers the risk in their eyes.

3. Applying Too Early

Timing matters. If you're two months into business with no steady revenue, banks don't care how passionate you are. They need proof, not promises.

A local landscaper I knew tried applying for a $50K line of credit after his first summer of work. He thought the "busy season" deposits were enough. The bank looked at the gaps in the off-season and said no. A year later, after showing steady contracts year-round, he applied again, and this time, approved.

Patience really does pay.

4. Asking for Too Much with No Proof

There's nothing wrong with shooting for the stars, but asking for $200K when your business is only pulling in $40K a year? That's like trying to deadlift 500 pounds when you've only been to the gym twice.

Start with what makes sense. If you can back up the ask with numbers, contracts, sales history, and projected growth, lenders listen. If not, they'll think you're unrealistic and shut the door fast.

5. Sloppy Paperwork

This one seems small, but it kills applications all the time. Mismatched addresses. Bank statements with missing pages. Business names are spelled differently on tax returns and licenses.

Lenders don't chase you down to fix it. They just move your file to the "denied" pile.

One entrepreneur I worked with got turned away three times for this exact reason. When she finally cleaned up her LLC paperwork, fixed her EIN registration, and double-checked her bank docs, the very same lender gave her the approval.

Key Takeaways: Building Your Funding Roadmap

By now, you've probably noticed, funding isn't about one big leap. It's about steps. Tiny, sometimes frustrating steps that eventually stack up into something powerful. The good news? If you treat it like a roadmap instead of a guessing game, you'll save yourself years of trial and error.

Step 1: Start Small (Secured Cards)

Think of secured cards as your learner's permit. You're not driving a Ferrari yet; you're just proving you know the basics. Drop $300–$1,000 as a deposit, use the card lightly, and pay it on time. Six to twelve months of this shows lenders you can handle responsibility.

A lot of people try to skip this stage. Don't. Even if you already have "okay" credit, starting with a secured card in your business's name builds the foundation you'll need later.

Step 2: Build the Habits That Matter

Funding isn't about fancy tricks. It's about boring, repeatable habits:

- Pay on time (every time).
- Keep balances under 30%.
- Separate your business and personal money.

Do those three things consistently, and lenders will start seeing you as a safe bet. Mess them up, and even a good credit score won't save you.

Step 3: Graduate to Bigger Tools

Once you've proven yourself with secured credit, you can move into unsecured business cards and eventually credit lines. This is the "graduation" moment. Limits jump from a few thousand to tens of thousands.

Most businesses take 12–18 months to reach this point. Some move faster if their revenue is steady and their paperwork is spotless. Others crawl because they mix personal and business expenses. The pace is in your hands.

Step 4: Package Yourself Like a Pro

Numbers alone don't close the deal. Lenders want the story too. That means:

- A one-page executive summary.
- Bank statements that actually make sense.
- A simple business plan (two pages is fine).
- A clear use-of-funds explanation.

When you hand a lender this neat, consistent package, you instantly separate yourself from the 80% of applicants who throw in messy documents and vague promises.

Step 5: Build Relationships Before You Need Them

Here's a trick almost no one talks about: get to know smaller banks and credit unions early. Open an account, say hi to the banker, and ask questions. Relationship-driven lenders often take more chances on businesses they *know*.

So when you're finally ready to apply, you're not just a file on their desk; you're that customer they've seen walk in every few weeks.

Step 6: Always Have Backup Options

Sometimes, despite your best efforts, the answer will still be no. That's when SBA microloans, online lenders, or credit unions come into play. They may cost a bit more, but they keep you moving forward instead of stuck in neutral.

Your 6–12 Month Roadmap

Let's put it all together:

Months 1–3:

- Open a secured card.
- Keep balances under 30%.
- Separate business/personal finances.

Months 4–6:

- Check personal and business credit.
- Clean up errors, pay down debts.
- Keep deposits consistent.

Months 7–12:

- Apply for unsecured business credit.
- Package your documents.
- Build relationships with small banks.
- Explore SBA/alternative options if needed.

Follow this track, and within a year, you'll have the foundation to chase serious funding without getting laughed out of the bank lobby.

Every step, from opening that first secured card to securing an SBA loan, is part of a ladder that takes your business from fragile beginnings to solid ground.

The key is consistency. Clean records, steady deposits, and a clear plan send the signal that you're not just chasing a dream, you're building something sustainable. Banks and lenders notice that.

Sarah's bakery and Mark's landscaping business prove the same point: start small, stay disciplined, and the doors to bigger opportunities open. What feels out of reach today can become possible tomorrow.

So instead of seeing funding as a hurdle, treat it as a staircase. Each payment, each approval, each new relationship with a lender is another step upward. Keep climbing, and soon you'll look back to realize you're not scraping by anymore, you're growing with confidence and control.

Chapter 08: Mistakes That Kill Your Credit

Nothing kills business credit faster than treating your company like a sidekick to your personal wallet. It might feel harmless, swiping the business card for groceries "just this once" or sliding a client payment into your personal checking account because it's easier, but to lenders, that's like showing up to a black-tie event in pajama pants. They instantly see your business as sloppy, unprofessional, and risky.

When you mix business and personal money, you blur the line between "you" and "your company." That means the whole point of building business credit, keeping your personal assets safe, starts to unravel. A lender, auditor, or even a court can argue, "Well, if they don't treat the business separately, why should we?" Suddenly, your personal savings, house, or paycheck are fair game if something goes wrong.

Here's the part most entrepreneurs underestimate: lenders don't need months of commingling to lose trust. Sometimes one messy bank statement is enough. What if you run a growing cleaning company? One week, you use your personal debit card to grab gas, groceries, and cleaning supplies. To you, it's all just life expenses. But when you apply for an equipment loan a few months later, the lender reviews your transactions. They don't see a thriving business; they see a tangled knot of personal and professional spending. That "minor slip" is enough to get your loan application tossed. Just like that, a $20 grocery run costs you a $20,000 growth opportunity.

The solution is straightforward but requires discipline. Open a dedicated business bank account and run every single business transaction through it. Pay yourself a salary or owner's draw, but never dip into business funds for personal bills. Think of your company as an entirely separate person; it earns, spends, and saves on its own. Your role is to manage it, not treat it like a personal piggy bank.

Does this sound strict? Maybe. But lenders love clean records. When they can trace expenses neatly, your credibility shoots up. A clean separation screams, "This is a serious operation." It tells them your business is stable, organized, and worthy of funding. And when you reach for bigger opportunities, credit lines, equipment loans, vendor accounts, you'll thank yourself for drawing that invisible, but vital, boundary.

The due date creeps up, the bill sits on the desk, and you think, *Eh, I'll handle it next week.* That one shrug can cost more than you realize. In the world of business credit, time is a ruthless judge. Thirty days late isn't just a slap on the wrist; it's a permanent mark that lenders keep circling back to whenever you ask for more money.

The clock starts ticking the moment you're late. At 30 days, it looks like you slipped up or hit a cash flow snag. That alone can ding your score and send a quiet message: "This business isn't always in control." Hit 60 days late, and things get uglier. Now your account is marked high risk, and lenders start questioning whether you can handle more credit at all. Push it to 90 days, and you're basically wearing a neon sign that says "default risk." Accounts can get shut down, collections might kick in, and good luck getting approved for anything serious in the future.

Imagine a trucking company with a solid reputation. Business is booming, trucks are busy, and the owner figures being a little late on the fuel card payment isn't a big deal. After all, it's just one bill. But when he applies for a fleet loan to expand, the lender pulls up his credit history. That single 60-day late payment overshadows years of on-time behavior. The application? Denied. One slip, massive consequences.

The frustrating part is how preventable it usually is. Automated payments take minutes to set up and can save years of headaches. Even if you only schedule the minimum payment, it keeps your record clean while you sort out the rest. Monitoring tools like Nav or CreditSafe make it easier too; they send alerts before small oversights snowball into disasters. And when cash really is tight, most vendors are surprisingly willing to work with you, as long as you reach out early. Silence gets you flagged; communication keeps doors open.

Think about how lenders view this cycle. They're not just looking at numbers on a report; they're watching behavior. Consistent on-time payments tell them you run a tight ship. Missed deadlines tell them you're juggling too much, even if the reality is more complicated. Every due date is a chance to show discipline, reliability, and respect for the credit system. Nail that, and lenders will be far more willing to back your growth when you need them most.

Swipe, swipe, swipe, it feels good in the moment, but that growing balance is telling lenders a different story. Credit utilization, the percentage of your available limit you're actually using, is one of the quiet killers in business credit. You might pay every bill on time, never miss a due date, and still end up looking like a risky bet simply because your balances are too high.

Lenders think in ranges, not excuses. Under 30% of your limit? You look stable and disciplined. Climbing past 50%? The warning lights start flashing. Hit 70% or more, and you might as well be waving a red flag. To them, a maxed-out card means you're desperate, strapped for cash, or seconds away from falling behind, even if that's not the full story.

A $7,500 balance doesn't sound scary until you realize it's sitting on a $10,000 limit. That's 75% utilization, and to a lender, it screams overextended. Contrast that with a $7,500 balance on a $50,000 limit, that same number suddenly looks like nothing. It's not the dollar amount that counts; it's the ratio, and too many business owners miss that detail until it comes back to bite them.

The good news is you don't need a magic wand to manage it; you just need a strategy. Spread purchases across multiple cards instead of loading everything onto one account. Request a higher credit limit once you've built some history; lenders often say yes if you've been paying on time. Pay balances down aggressively before the statement date, so the utilization they report is lower than what you actually carried during the month: small moves, big perception shifts.

Think of utilization as body language for your business finances. You could be profitable, organized, and fully in control, but if your credit report shows maxed-out accounts, lenders see stress and instability. Keep it light, keep it under control, and you'll come across as a business that knows how to handle growth without drowning in debt.

The lesson is simple: utilization isn't just math, it's a story about how you manage resources. Stay under the thresholds, and that story is one of discipline and balance. Cross into the danger zones, and the same numbers suddenly read like panic. Which version do you want lenders to believe?

The Trap of Personal Guarantees

Signing a personal guarantee feels harmless at first. The bank slides the paper across the desk. You're eager to get funding, and the fine print says you'll back the loan with your own name. Most owners shrug it off. After all, it's just paperwork. But that small signature can quietly tie your personal life to every bump your business hits.

A personal guarantee means the lender isn't really betting on your company; they're betting on you. If the business stumbles, your savings, home equity, and even your paycheck can be on the line. It defeats the whole purpose of building business credit in the first place, which is to create a firewall between you and the company. Instead of that shield, you're volunteering to take the hit if things go sideways.

The danger shows up when owners rely on personal guarantees long after they've outgrown them. Early on, they're almost unavoidable. Vendors and banks want reassurance before extending credit to a new business with no track record. Signing makes sense in the beginning. The trap is staying locked into those agreements once your business profile is strong enough to stand on its own.

Take the restaurant owner who signed a $50,000 equipment loan with a personal guarantee. When sales dipped and the restaurant closed, the lender didn't chase the business. They went straight after the owner. That one contract dragged him into personal bankruptcy, even though the company had been incorporated to protect him. The business failed, but the damage followed him home.

Breaking out of this cycle means being intentional. Use PG-backed accounts early to establish history, but transition out as soon as your credit profile allows. Vendors like Uline or Quill often start with PG terms, but they'll remove them once you've proven consistency. Larger lenders will, too, if you've built up enough trust. The key is asking and moving forward, not passively renewing the same risky agreements year after year.

Personal guarantees are like training wheels. They help at the start, but if you keep them on forever, they'll slow you down and wreck you in a crash. The faster you build your profile and graduate into non-PG accounts, the safer your personal finances will be, and the more real independence your business will have.

Behavior Over Numbers – How Lenders Really Judge

Most business owners obsess over the score. They watch every point tick up or down, thinking that number alone will decide their future. Lenders don't actually work that way. They care about behavior, the patterns behind the numbers, far more than the digits on a report.

Think about it from their perspective. A credit score is just a snapshot, like one frame out of a movie. Behavior tells the whole film. Paying on time every month, keeping balances under control, separating business from personal finances, those consistent habits matter more than chasing a perfect number. A lender would rather see a "good" score backed by steady, disciplined behavior than a "great" score built on shaky habits.

It's easy to underestimate how closely they pay attention. That one late payment doesn't just drop your score; it raises a question: Does this business cut corners when things get tough? Running a maxed-out balance doesn't just affect utilization; it tells a story that you might be running on fumes. Commingling business and personal accounts isn't just sloppy; it signals you're not treating your company as a real entity. These aren't math errors; they're behavior red flags.

What lenders want to see is boring reliability. A business that pays when it should, spends responsibly, and keeps clean records. Boring is beautiful to a lender because it means less risk. They're not looking for a flashy operator who spikes their score with quick fixes; they're looking for someone who treats credit like a tool, not a gamble.

This is the part many entrepreneurs get wrong. They think one clever trick will "game" the system. In reality, nothing builds credibility faster than quiet discipline. Auto-payments, tidy account separation, manageable balances, those small, consistent moves compound into a reputation that lenders trust. And when you need bigger opportunities, like equipment financing or a major line of credit, that trust pays off.

Numbers will always matter, but they're only the surface. What lenders are really measuring is how you act when nobody's watching. Do you treat credit like a lifeline or like a lever for growth? Do you take shortcuts or show discipline? The patterns tell the truth, and the truth decides who gets funded and who gets passed over.

Chapter 09: Leveraging Your Credit For Growth

Funding Options That Unlock Growth

One of the biggest turning points for a business comes when credit stops being a safety net and starts becoming a growth engine. At the very beginning, credit feels like survival; you use a small card here, maybe a personal loan there, just to cover the bills and keep operations moving. But once you've built real business credit, something changes. Banks, lenders, and even suppliers start to treat you differently. You're no longer in the position of pleading for help; you're choosing from a menu of powerful financial tools.

That shift is everything. With strong credit, you unlock options that were once out of reach. You gain the ability to expand without draining your own savings, to hire without worrying about payroll gaps, to invest in opportunities when they arrive instead of watching them slip by. In short, credit becomes leverage.

Let's break down the most impactful ways to fund growth once your business is creditworthy, not in theory, but in practical terms you can actually use.

The Power of SBA Loans

If business credit is your foundation, SBA loans are the skyscrapers you can build on top of it. The SBA, or Small Business Administration, doesn't directly lend you money; instead, it guarantees part of the loan for the bank. That guarantee lowers the risk for lenders, which means they can offer you more favorable terms.

Here's why this matters: with an SBA loan, you can often borrow larger amounts, lock in lower interest rates, and spread repayment out over longer periods. That's the holy trinity of growth financing: more money, cheaper cost, less pressure.

Imagine a local restaurant that's built a loyal customer base in one neighborhood. They dream of opening a second location, but the upfront costs, leasing, renovations, hiring staff, and marketing are overwhelming. Without funding, that dream stays stuck on paper. With solid credit and a strong business plan, they qualify for an SBA loan. Suddenly, expansion isn't just possible, it's manageable. They get the funds they need on terms that allow them to repay comfortably as the new location begins to generate revenue.

That's the difference between business credit in theory and business credit in action. It transforms what feels impossible into a realistic next step.

Lines of Credit: The Flexible Safety Net

If an SBA loan is like a mortgage for your business growth, a line of credit is more like a high-powered toolkit. It doesn't lock you into one lump-sum loan. Instead, it's revolving, which means you can borrow, repay, and borrow again. You only pay interest on what you use, and it's always there when you need it.

This flexibility is a lifeline, especially for businesses with uneven cash flow. Picture a landscaping company gearing up for spring. Spring is their busiest season, but it also requires heavy upfront investment: ordering mulch, renting equipment, and hiring extra staff. Without capital, they risk losing contracts to competitors who can afford to move faster. A $50,000 line of credit changes the game. They stock up, meet demand, and then repay the credit once the revenue rolls in.

The beauty of a line of credit is that it gives you breathing room. It prevents missed opportunities, late payrolls, and frantic scrambles for cash. And because you're leveraging credit you've already built, the terms are usually far better than those predatory "quick loan" offers that trap so many businesses.

Equipment Financing: Scaling Without Sacrificing Cash Flow

Every industry has its tools. For some, it's machinery; for others, it's vehicles, computers, or medical devices. The problem? Equipment is expensive. Paying for it outright can wipe out your cash reserves, leaving you vulnerable. That's where equipment financing steps in.

With equipment financing, you don't have to choose between upgrading your tools and protecting your cash flow. The loan or lease is tied directly to the equipment, which often serves as collateral. This reduces the lender's risk and makes financing more accessible for businesses with good credit.

Take a printing company as an example. They've been operating with older presses, but a new high-capacity digital press could double their output and open doors to bigger clients. The price tag is steep, hundreds of thousands of dollars. Paying cash would leave them exposed. Instead, they finance the press. Monthly payments are manageable, and the new revenue they generate more than covers the cost. Within a year, their profits grow by 40%.

This is how credit fuels transformation: by letting you make bold moves today that pay off tomorrow.

Invoice Factoring: Turning Waiting Into Opportunity

One of the most frustrating parts of running a business is waiting for clients to pay. You can deliver a project worth $100,000, but if your client pays on net-60 terms, you're stuck waiting two months to see that money. Meanwhile, bills are due, opportunities arise, and you don't have the cash to move.

Invoice factoring flips that script. Instead of waiting, you sell your invoices to a lender for immediate cash. They advance you most of the value upfront (often 80–90%), and when your client finally pays, the lender takes their cut and returns the rest.

Consider a marketing agency that just finished a massive campaign for a corporate client. The invoice is $120,000, but payment won't arrive for 90 days. The agency needs funds now to hire freelancers for two new projects. By factoring the invoice, they get the cash immediately, keep their momentum, and take on more work instead of slowing down.

Some business owners hesitate at factoring because it reduces the total they receive. But the reality is this: having $100,000 in three months is often worth less than having $90,000 today. With credit in your corner, you're not waiting around; you're moving forward.

Other Options Worth Knowing

Beyond these main tools, there are additional ways to leverage credit for growth:

- **Vendor Credit:** Agreements like net-30 or net-60 terms let you buy supplies now and pay later, which helps free up cash flow and build your credit profile at the same time.
- **Merchant Cash Advances:** These provide quick funding against future sales. They're expensive and should be used sparingly, but for short-term emergencies, they can be a bridge.
- **Crowdfunding & Peer-to-Peer Lending:** These newer, flexible options combine business credibility with community support or investor backing. They can be especially powerful for startups with strong branding or customer loyalty.

Bringing It All Together

The lesson here isn't that one funding option is better than another; it's that each serves a different role. An SBA loan fuels major expansions. A line of credit smooths cash flow. Equipment financing unlocks new capacity. Invoice factoring keeps momentum when clients are slow to pay. Vendor credit and alternative funding fill the gaps.

The common thread? None of these doors open without strong business credit. Without it, you're stuck with high-interest loans, limited approval, and constant financial stress. With it, you have the freedom to choose the right tool for the right moment.

That's what leveraging credit really means: turning money you don't yet have into opportunities you couldn't otherwise afford, and doing it strategically so that every borrowed dollar multiplies into more.

Understanding and Maximizing Business Buying Power

Here's the thing nobody really tells you: having credit is one thing, but knowing how to *use it like a weapon* in business? That's a whole different game. Most entrepreneurs think of credit as just "money to borrow." But when you build strong business credit, what you really gain is buying power, and that's the secret sauce for growth.

Buying power isn't just about how much cash or credit you can access. It's about the leverage that comes with it. The bigger your buying power, the more seriously suppliers, lenders, and even partners take you. It changes the tone of every conversation. Instead of asking for favors, you're negotiating deals. Instead of paying retail, you're locking in discounts. Instead of waiting in line, you're moving to the front.

Why Buying Power Matters

Let's get real. Business is expensive. Inventory costs pile up. Vendors want their cut. Equipment breaks down. Opportunities pop up at the worst possible times. Without buying power, you're constantly reactive, scrambling for cash, stretching credit cards, juggling bills.

But with established credit, your buying power gives you room to breathe. It lets you say yes when opportunity knocks, instead of "I wish I could."

Imagine you run a boutique clothing store. A supplier offers you a bulk order deal on the hottest seasonal items at a 20% discount, but only if you can pay upfront. If you have credit lines available, you should jump on them. That one move could double your profit margins for the season. Without buying power? You miss out, and your competitors stock the shelves instead.

The Supplier Advantage

One of the most underrated perks of good credit is how it transforms your relationship with suppliers. When suppliers know you can handle bigger orders, they're more willing to extend better terms. Instead of paying everything up front, you might get net-30, net-60, or even net-90 deals. That's basically like getting an interest-free loan directly from your supplier.

And here's where it gets fun: the more reliable you are in paying, the more those terms improve. Before you know it, you're buying larger volumes, paying later, and getting better prices. That's not just convenience, that's growth fuel.

Negotiating From Strength

Buying power also changes how you negotiate. Credit is credibility. When you walk into a meeting with suppliers or lenders, and they see your strong business credit profile, they know you're reliable. That shifts the power dynamic. You're not begging for help, you're offering them business.

And when you negotiate from strength, you get perks:

- Lower interest rates.
- Higher credit limits.
- Discounts for bulk purchases.
- Faster approvals.

This is where a lot of business owners miss out. They think, *"Well, I got approved, that's enough."* But the real move is asking for more, and credit gives you the leverage to do that.

Protecting and Growing Your Buying Power

Buying power isn't a one-and-done deal. You've got to protect it and grow it, just like any other asset.

That means:

- **Keep utilization low.** Don't max out every credit line; lenders like to see space.
- **Pay early, not just on time.** Early payments signal strength.
- **Diversify credit.** Mix of credit cards, lines, vendor accounts, loans = a healthier profile.
- **Review your limits often.** Don't be shy about asking lenders to raise your limits as your business grows.

Think of buying power like a muscle. Use it wisely, build it consistently, and it only gets stronger. Abuse it, and it weakens fast.

Big Picture: From Buyer to Player

The real magic of buying power is that it flips your role in the market. You're no longer just a buyer; you become a player. You set terms, you make strategic moves, and you're able to take advantage of opportunities most small businesses miss.

When your credit is strong, and your buying power is sharp, you're not just running a business, you're running the business on your terms. And that's where the path to real growth begins.

Using Credit Strategically for Real Growth

Here's the truth: a lot of business owners get credit, but then they waste it. They treat it like a backup wallet, something to swipe when they're short on cash. That's not strategy, that's survival. If you want to build real wealth with your business, you've got to flip the way you think about credit.

Credit is leverage. And when you use it intentionally, it's the fastest way to grow without waiting ten years to "save up."

Operations vs. Growth: Big Difference

There's a huge difference between using credit for operations and using it for growth.

- **Operations** = paying bills, covering payroll, and keeping the lights on. That's fine in emergencies, but it doesn't multiply your money.
- **Growth** = using credit to fund something that will *generate more revenue* in return. That's where the magic happens.

Think about it: swiping a business card to pay your utility bill? Necessary sometimes, sure, but that doesn't build wealth. Taking out a credit line to buy a new delivery van that doubles your capacity? That's credit paying for itself.

Real Estate Moves

Many entrepreneurs don't realize that business credit can extend to real estate, whether that involves buying your own office space, leasing with more favorable terms, or even investing in a small property to rent out as additional income.

Let's say you're paying crazy rent for your store. With solid credit, you qualify for financing to actually buy a small commercial space. Suddenly, instead of burning money on rent every month, you're building equity. Over time, that equity can be borrowed against for future growth. That's a strategic play.

Equipment That Pays for Itself

We touched on equipment financing earlier, but here's the strategic angle: don't buy equipment just to replace old gear. Use credit to buy equipment that makes you more money.

A local bakery invests in an industrial oven. It's not just replacing the old one; it triples baking capacity. That means more bread on shelves, more wholesale contracts, and more revenue. Within months, the equipment is paying itself off, and then it's pure profit.

That's the mindset shift: don't borrow for what keeps you the same. Borrow for what makes you grow.

Acquiring Other Businesses

This one sounds big, and it is, but it's also way more doable than most people think. Business credit can be used to acquire a competitor, merge with a smaller company, or buy out a struggling business with valuable assets.

Scaling Up the Smart Way

Don't just throw credit at random opportunities. Timing and planning matter.

Ask yourself:

- Does this investment create new income?

- Can I realistically repay it with that new income?
- What's the risk if things go slower than planned?

If you can answer those three questions and the math works out, you're not taking on debt; you're investing with leverage. That's what separates the business owners who spin their wheels from the ones who break through to the next level.

The ROI Mindset

Think of every dollar of borrowed credit like a seed. If you plant it in the right place, it grows into a tree that produces fruit for years. If you scatter it on concrete (like bills that don't bring a return), it dies.

That's the mindset shift strategic entrepreneurs make: they stop seeing credit as "money owed" and start seeing it as "money multiplied."

Credit is for building ladders. Use it with intention, use it for growth moves that pay back more than you borrowed, and suddenly, credit stops being scary. It becomes exciting.

Because here's the secret: the businesses that scale fast aren't always the ones with the most sales. They're the ones who know how to leverage credit strategically to take big steps when others are still saving up for baby ones.

Timing Is Everything (And So Is Playing It Smart)

Here's the deal: credit isn't some magic wand you wave whenever you feel like it. You've got to know when to pull the trigger. Get the timing wrong, and you're stuck paying off debt for moves that never paid back. Get it right, and credit becomes rocket fuel.

The Danger of "Too Soon"

A lot of entrepreneurs get excited the minute they qualify for a line of credit. Suddenly, they're swiping for everything: a shiny new office, expensive branding, extra staff. But if your cash flow isn't steady yet? That's a disaster waiting to happen.

Think of it like lifting weights: if you load up the bar too soon, you'll get crushed. Build the strength first (a.k.a. consistent revenue), *then* start stacking the weight (a.k.a. bigger credit plays).

The Trap of "Too Late"

On the flip side, some business owners wait forever. They keep saying, *"I'll invest when the time is perfect."* Guess what? The perfect time never shows up.

Example: A catering business waits too long to get a credit line for a second food truck. By the time they're ready, a competitor has already swooped in, parked their trucks all over town, and captured the market.

Moral of the story: waiting can be just as risky as rushing.

The Sweet Spot

So when's the right time? Usually it's when:

1. You've got steady sales coming in (not crazy growth, just consistency).
2. You've spotted an opportunity that won't wait forever (new location, contract, bulk order, whatever).

3. The return on that opportunity is bigger than the cost of credit.

That's your green light.

Have a Game Plan Before You Swipe

Here's where most business owners mess up: they get the funding first, and *then* they try to figure out what to do with it. That's backwards.

Do it like this instead:

- **Step 1:** Spot the opportunity (bigger space, new equipment, new market).
- **Step 2:** Run the numbers. What's the cost? What's the payoff? How long until it pays itself back?
- **Step 3:** Line up your plan, *then* go get the credit.

It sounds simple, but trust me, having a plan before you borrow is the difference between building an empire and digging a financial grave.

Risk Isn't the Enemy, Ignorance Is

Every investment carries risk. That's just life. The real problem is when you dive in blind. Good business owners don't avoid risk; they manage it.

How?

- **Diversify:** Don't put all your borrowed money into one move. Spread it.
- **Safety Net:** Keep some credit unused for emergencies.

- **Exit Strategy:** Ask yourself, "What if this flops? How do I cover it without sinking the whole ship?"

The Long Game Mindset

Here's the truth: leveraging credit isn't about winning quick. It's about building stability over time. If your plan relies on "blowing up overnight," it's not a plan, it's a gamble.

Instead, focus on moves that compound. A new machine that cuts costs every month. A location that doubles foot traffic for years. A supplier deal that saves 10% on every order. Those wins stack up, and credit just speeds up the process.

Credit as a Wealth-Building Tool (Not Just a Band-Aid)

Most business owners only think of credit as "help when cash is low." That's a survival mindset, and survival mode will keep you small. The real game? Using credit to move past the day-to-day grind and actually build wealth that lasts.

Beyond Bills and Band-Aids

Paying bills, covering gaps, patching holes, that's credit on training wheels. Nothing wrong with it, but it's not wealth-building. True leverage is when credit fuels something permanent: assets, ownership, or expansion.

Think: not "how do I keep the lights on this month?" but "how do I build something that'll pay me for years?"

From Operations to Ownership

At some point, you've got to shift focus from just "running the business" to "owning assets that make the business stronger." Credit makes that shift possible.

That might mean buying the building your store operates in, investing in systems that cut costs forever, or locking down supplier terms that boost profit margins long-term.

The Compounding Effect

The smartest use of credit is stacking small moves that keep paying back. A better deal with a supplier, a machine that cuts production costs, a system that automates work. Each one might not feel huge, but over time, they compound into serious gains.

Credit is just the accelerator; it lets you grab those opportunities now instead of years later.

Long-Term Freedom, Not Just Growth

Growth is great, but freedom is the real goal. You don't want to be chained to a business that only survives if you grind harder every year.

When credit is used to secure wealth-building moves, assets, equity, and smart acquisitions, you're setting yourself up for independence. That means the business works for you, not the other way around.

Credit can keep your business afloat, sure. But if that's all you ever use it for, you're missing the bigger picture. The real power comes when you use credit to build things that last, assets, systems, and wealth. That's how you stop playing defense and start playing offense with your business future.

Chapter 10: Automating Success

The simple act of putting things on autopilot can change everything. Bills get paid on time, reports get monitored, and your finances stay organized without you having to chase every little detail. It's not about being lazy; it's about being smart. Because in business, missed deadlines or forgotten payments can quietly kill your credit, no matter how hard you work.

Automation takes out the one thing that makes most people slip, human error. We all forget things sometimes. You get busy, an invoice slips through the cracks, or you assume you already paid something. Then suddenly, that one late payment shows up on your credit report like a stain that's hard to wash off. When your system runs automatically, those mistakes just stop happening. Payments go out, reminders get triggered, alerts pop up before a problem grows too big to fix. You end up saving not just time, but your reputation too.

And there's something deeply comforting about knowing things are handled. You're not waking up at 3 a.m., wondering if you missed a due date or if your account's off by a few hundred dollars. The background noise of worry goes quiet. Instead of living in constant reaction mode, you start running your business from a place of calm. Automation brings that quiet confidence; it gives you mental space to actually think, to plan, to grow.

The truth is, credit health isn't built in one big move; it's built in small, consistent actions. Automation keeps those actions consistent even on your busiest days. It's like having an invisible partner who remembers everything and never forgets a date. You stay ahead of issues, catch red flags early, and free yourself to focus on what really matters: growth, strategy, and the parts of your business that actually inspire you.

Once you put the right systems in place, the chaos starts to fade. You're no longer chasing bills or patching mistakes; you're leading your business with rhythm and order. And that's where real credit strength begins, not in constant effort, but in quiet consistency.

Once you understand the power of automation, the next step is choosing the right tools to make it all work smoothly. The truth is, no matter how disciplined you are, trying to track every payment, monitor your credit score, and manage daily expenses manually will eventually wear you down. That's where technology steps in. These tools are like your behind-the-scenes team, quiet, reliable, and always awake.

Let's start with *credit monitoring.* Keeping an eye on your credit shouldn't be something you only do when things go wrong. It should be part of your regular business rhythm. Platforms like *CreditSafe* give you detailed business credit reports, risk ratings, and instant alerts if anything changes in your profile. Whether it's a new inquiry or a slight drop in score, you'll know before it turns into something serious.

Then there's *NAV*, which is one of my personal favorites because it pulls everything together. It tracks your Experian, Equifax, and Dun & Bradstreet business scores all in one simple dashboard. You can see where you stand at a glance instead of jumping between different websites. NAV even recommends funding options based on your profile, which can save you time and open doors you didn't even know existed.

Dun & Bradstreet's Credit Monitor, sometimes called the gold standard of business credit, lets you track trade lines, your PAYDEX score, and any updates to your business file. These little details matter. One missed or outdated record can make a lender question your reliability. Having a system that updates automatically keeps your profile clean and accurate.

Now, when it comes to *bookkeeping and expense tracking*, this is where automation truly shines. Tools like *QuickBooks Online* and *Xero* are lifesavers. They automatically sync with your bank account, categorize transactions, and generate reports without you having to touch a calculator. *Wave* is another solid option, especially for small businesses. It's free and handles invoices, bill payments, and receipts in one simple platform.

If you're managing multiple vendors or recurring bills, *Bill.com* and *Melio* make life easier. You can schedule payments, set up recurring ones, and even pay suppliers by credit card while they receive ACH or checks, whichever they prefer. That flexibility keeps everyone happy and your payments always on time.

Then there's *Divvy*, which combines business credit cards with built-in expense management and budget automation. It's like having a financial assistant that not only tracks spending but also enforces discipline. You can assign budgets, set limits, and review everything from one dashboard.

All of these tools work best when they're connected. When your bookkeeping software talks to your bank, which then talks to your credit monitor, your entire financial picture stays aligned. Everything updates automatically, errors drop, and your records stay clean. And clean records aren't just nice to have, they're your silent armor when lenders or investors take a closer look at your business.

In the end, these systems don't just save you from chaos; they buy you freedom. Freedom from stress, from manual errors, from the endless mental clutter of remembering who to pay and when. Once your finances start syncing like clockwork, you can finally breathe a little easier and focus on the parts of your business that actually light you up.

Automation can take you far, but it can't do everything. You still need human eyes, human instincts, and that touch of experience that only comes with years of dealing with numbers, clients, and unexpected messes. The truth is, the best systems are the ones where technology and people work together, machines handle the routine, and humans handle the judgment calls. That balance keeps your financial world both smooth and smart.

Even the most advanced software can't look at your books and say, *"Hey, something feels off here."* That's what a good *bookkeeper* does. They're the ones making sure every dollar in and out is properly recorded, that your accounts reconcile, and your books actually reflect your real financial health. Bookkeepers keep your system clean day to day. They catch small mistakes before they snowball into something ugly. Think of them as your first line of defense.

Then there are *accountants*, the big-picture thinkers. They don't just handle taxes; they help you plan, strategize, and make smarter decisions. A good accountant can tell you when to borrow, when to reinvest, or when to just hold steady. They make sure your business stays compliant and that every deduction, every credit, and every move you make is backed by solid reasoning. They're the ones who turn all that data your software collects into an actual growth strategy.

And finally, we have *credit specialists*. These are the people who understand how business credit really works, the scoring, the tiers, the vendors that report, and the ones that don't. They guide you through setting up accounts that actually build your credit, not just look busy on paper. If there's an error on your credit report, they know how to dispute it. If you're trying to move up from starter accounts to higher-tier financing, they'll map the path for you. Some business owners hire credit specialists short-term basis, just for 90 days, to build a strong foundation, and then maintain things themselves afterward. It's a smart move if you're just getting started or trying to clean up old damage.

When you bring these professionals into your system, you're not just outsourcing work; you're buying peace of mind. You're creating a structure that holds itself together even when life gets chaotic. Bookkeepers handle the details, accountants manage the plan, and credit specialists make sure your reputation with lenders stays strong. Together, they keep everything compliant, optimized, and running like a well-oiled machine.

A few tips from experience: when hiring, look for people who already use modern tools like QuickBooks or Xero. That way, your data stays cloud-based and accessible anytime you need it. Ask questions, too. You want people who explain things in plain language, not financial jargon. The best professionals make you feel more confident, not more confused.

At the end of the day, automation might run your systems, but people give it life. The right mix of both builds a foundation that's solid, reliable, and ready for growth. When you surround yourself with experts who care about the details, you free yourself to focus on what really matters, leading your business forward without the constant worry of what's happening behind the scenes.

Once you've got the right tools and the right people, the final step is creating a system that almost runs itself, a true "set it and forget it" setup. The kind of system where your bills get paid, your reports stay clean, and your credit keeps growing even when you're not constantly checking it. That's the sweet spot. You're not reacting anymore, you're in control, quietly and confidently.

Start with automation for payments and cash flow, because nothing damages credit faster than late payments. Set up *auto-pay* for all your business credit cards, at least for the minimum due, so nothing slips through the cracks. Link your business checking account to your lenders and use bank alerts to warn you before any overdrafts or large transactions. Tools like Bill.com and Melio make it simple to pay vendors and suppliers right on schedule. You can even use credit cards to make payments, while the other side receives ACH or checks; it's smooth and keeps everyone happy.

Next, handle *payroll automation*. Systems like *Gusto* or *ADP* take care of payroll and keep you tax compliant without all the headaches. Lenders like seeing a stable payroll; it shows reliability. Every steady paycheck sent out builds quiet trust in your business's consistency.

Beyond payments, you need constant eyes on your credit, because small mistakes can grow fast. Automated monitoring from tools like *CreditSafe* or *NAV* keeps you informed. You'll get alerts when your score changes, when a new inquiry appears, or if a vendor reports a late payment by mistake. That kind of early warning system can save you from unnecessary damage. Even simple *bank text alerts* for deposits and withdrawals help you spot something strange before it turns into a problem.

And don't forget the *dashboard view.* Programs like *QuickBooks* or *Xero* give you real-time snapshots of your financial health. One look, and you can see your cash flow, invoices, and expenses without flipping through spreadsheets. When all your accounts, banks, cards, and credit monitors feed into a single central hub, your financial life becomes clearer and more manageable.

Now, here's the trick that keeps it all easy: *review monthly, not daily.* Spend one focused hour each month going through reports, checking alerts, and making minor adjustments if needed. The rest of the time, let your system do its job. The point of automation isn't to make you more obsessed with your money, it's to give you freedom from it.

Assign roles where needed. Your *bookkeeper* handles daily entries, your *accountant* handles tax and planning, and your *credit specialist* deals with disputes or updates. Each one plays a part, but your role shifts from "doing everything" to just *overseeing* everything. That's how real businesses grow, with structure, not chaos.

Over time, you'll start to notice something: less stress, fewer surprises, more control. The calls about missed payments stop coming. Your credit reports start looking cleaner. You actually have space to think about the future instead of constantly fixing the past.

Automation doesn't just protect your credit; it protects your peace. It shields you from the everyday noise and frees your mind to focus on growth. Because when your systems are working quietly in the background, you get to put your energy where it truly belongs, on expanding, creating, and leading.

So, if you take one thing from this chapter, let it be this: *build your financial world to run even when you're not watching.* Automate what you can, hire smart where it matters, and check in just enough to stay informed. When your credit, cash flow, and payments move in sync, business stops feeling like a juggling act and starts feeling like a rhythm.

That's when you know your credit and your business are finally on autopilot.

Conclusion: The Blueprint To Wealth Starts Here

Every journey begins with a single step. When we started out, we didn't have all the answers, and certainly not the resources we have now. We didn't understand business credit, we didn't have access to endless funding, and we didn't fully grasp how systems could transform chaos into structure. But as we built Exclusive Whips Automotive, City Lounge, and SoDelicious, we uncovered something powerful, a system for building wealth that anyone can follow if they're willing to commit to the process.

This book has been that system, broken down step by step. It's a map, a manual, and a mirror all at once. You've learned how to form a legitimate business, how to establish credit lines, how to leverage funding for expansion, and how to automate operations for scalability. You now hold the same blueprint we used to turn our ideas into thriving, credit-backed companies. And as we close this second volume, we're not just summarizing information, we're solidifying a new way of thinking.

Once you truly understand business credit, you'll never see money or opportunity the same way again.

Laying the Foundation

You started by learning the basics, how to build a foundation that commands respect from lenders and partners alike. Registering your LLC, setting up your EIN, and securing a professional address, phone number, and email. These may have felt like small, bureaucratic steps, but they are the bedrock of credibility. Banks, vendors, and investors recognize legitimacy through these formalities. They signal that you're serious, structured, and ready for business.

Then came those first small credit accounts. Maybe it didn't seem like much, ordering supplies on net-30 terms, paying invoices on time, keeping balances low. But those humble beginnings are what opened the door to everything that followed. That first trade line isn't just a number; it's a vote of confidence from the financial system.

Leveraging Credit for Growth

Once your business credit profile was established, the game changed. Suddenly, funding options expanded. You learned about SBA loans, equipment financing, microloans, invoice factoring, and business lines of credit, each a powerful tool to grow without touching your personal savings. This was the moment your business stopped depending on your wallet and started standing on its own financial legs.

Through these pages, you learned how to use these tools strategically, not recklessly. Funding is fuel, but only when it's managed with discipline. It's not about chasing loans; it's about using leverage to multiply opportunity. That's what we did with our ventures, and that's what this blueprint empowers you to do too.

Automating and Scaling

The final key in this system is automation, turning chaos into control. You discovered how tools like credit monitoring, bookkeeping software, CRM systems, social media schedulers, and inventory management platforms save you time, reduce errors, and create space for growth.

Automation isn't just convenience, it's capacity. It allows you to focus on leadership, innovation, and expansion rather than drowning in daily tasks. It's the difference between working *in* your business and working *on* your business. Each automated system becomes another piece of your financial engine, running smoothly even while you rest.

The Interconnected System

Every concept in this book connects to the next. Business structure leads to credibility. Credibility unlocks credit. Credit enables funding. Funding fuels growth. Growth demands automation. Each builds upon the last; each is a rung in the ladder of financial independence. Skip one, and the structure weakens. Follow them all, and the system becomes self-sustaining.

That's the secret we discovered through trial and error: wealth is built by systems, not by luck.

We began as hustlers, working endlessly to make ends meet. But when we applied this blueprint, we became business owners, leaders with scalable, automated, and credit-backed enterprises. You can do the same.

Beyond Money: Building a Legacy

This blueprint isn't just about making money; it's about creating something that lasts. Anyone can chase a paycheck. What we're building is legacy.

Strong business credit is more than access to funding; it's an asset in itself. A company with an established credit profile is *worth more*. It can be sold for a higher price, expanded more easily, or passed down to the next generation already equipped for success.

Think of it: when your children inherit your company, they inherit not just the brand and assets, but the financial credibility you built. They start where you left off, on solid ground, with open doors and strong relationships already in place.

And it doesn't stop with family. Business credit empowers you to give back, creating jobs, offering mentorship, and stimulating your community's economy. That's what City Lounge, Exclusive Whips Automotive, and SoDelicious came to represent for us. They're more than profitable ventures; they're proof that disciplined strategy can turn dreams into generational stability.

Generational wealth doesn't begin with millions; it begins with knowledge. And now, you have that knowledge.

The Blueprint Mindset

The biggest transformation we experienced wasn't financial; it was mental. We went from saying, *"We can't afford this,"* to asking, *"How can we use credit to fund this?"* That single shift changed everything.

At City Lounge, we used business credit to renovate immediately instead of saving for years, and doubled our revenue. At Exclusive

Whips Automotive, we financed equipment that paid for itself within months. At SoDelicious, we invested in catering gear that opened the door to large-scale contracts.

This mindset doesn't just accelerate growth; it protects you. With strong business credit, you never have to risk your personal savings again. You never have to put your own financial future on the line to keep your dream alive. That's the Blueprint Mindset: turning every challenge into an opportunity.

Facing Challenges with Strategy

Let's be real, challenges will come. Not every loan application will get approved. Some customers will pay late. Some automation systems won't work perfectly the first time.

But with this blueprint, setbacks become strategy sessions. A denied loan becomes a reason to strengthen your credit profile. A late customer payment becomes an opportunity to explore invoice factoring. Too much workload? Time to delegate or automate.

We faced all of these challenges, and every single one became a stepping stone. The same will be true for you if you view every obstacle as data, every mistake as a lesson.

The Power of Financial Legacy

One of the most powerful truths we learned is that business credit outlives the owner.

If you sell your company, its credit profile goes with it, instantly increasing its market value. If you pass it down, your heirs inherit more than a business; they inherit a financially credible enterprise. That's the essence of legacy: creating something that continues to generate value even when you step away.

Your business credit can open doors for generations to come, doors that were once closed to you. Stability, opportunity, and security become transferable. That's the power of this system.

Reflecting on Your Journey

Think back to when you first opened this book. Maybe you were uncertain. Maybe "business credit" felt abstract or intimidating. But now, you've walked through the entire process, from setting up your foundation to securing real funding, to automating for scale, and finally, to building wealth that endures.

That transformation proves something simple yet profound: you have what it takes. You're not just capable of running a business, you're capable of creating a financial ecosystem that supports your dreams and your family's future.

Your Blueprint for True Financial Freedom

Here's the ultimate takeaway: with this blueprint, you never have to risk your personal money for business purposes again. You now understand how to fund growth using O.P.M., Other People's Money, and how to protect your personal credit and assets while doing so.

You have the tools to build scalable systems, the knowledge to sustain them, and the mindset to keep expanding. This isn't just about starting a business; it's about building a self-sustaining engine that funds itself and pays you back over time.

With this blueprint, you are not just surviving, you are thriving, expanding, and leading.

Final Words of Motivation

The world is yours.

Building business credit isn't just about dollars and cents; it's about confidence, opportunity, and freedom. It's about walking into a bank knowing you have the profile lenders respect. It's about negotiating with suppliers from a position of strength. It's about protecting your family's future while building your dream in the present.

We built City Lounge, Exclusive Whips Automotive, and SoDelicious using this very blueprint. We lived it, refined it, and saw the results firsthand. And now, the same path is open to you.

You are ready to turn challenges into opportunities. You are ready to transform ideas into thriving enterprises. You are ready to build not just a business, but a financial legacy that will outlast you.

The blueprint is in your hands.

The wealth starts now.

About the Author

David Washington is an entrepreneur, investor, and financial strategist committed to helping people break free from traditional limitations and build generational wealth through business credit. With hands-on experience running multiple companies, navigating real estate, and developing business systems from the ground up, David offers a direct, practical approach to achieving financial success.

His mission is simple: teach people how to leverage credit, not cash, to grow their businesses, protect their assets, and regain their financial freedom.

Through his books, coaching, and personal journey, David empowers others to think bigger, move strategically, and understand the true power of building wealth the right way without risking their own money.

www.ingramcontent.com/pod-product-compliance
Lightning Source LLC
LaVergne TN
LVHW050916210926
848482LV00012B/462